Praise

"This book is a wonderful gift to parents! Ms. Benchimol writes with clear experience and wisdom about how to interact with children in ways that best nurture their growth and development across important domains such as boundaries, communication, and learning. The communication of knowledge in bite-sized 'pearls' that are easily read and digested by busy parents will make this book a trusted and favored parenting tool. Ms. Benchimol's brief and brilliant advice offers concrete strategies to increase compassion, authenticity, and joy in everyday life, while reflecting a deep sense of understanding and respect for a child's independence and unique gifts. She shares with clarity her love, passion, and expertise for nurturing children during the critical developmental period of early childhood. This book is a must read!"

— Amy E. West, Ph.D., Clinical Child Psychologist

Pearls for Parents' Happiness

"Brigitte Benchimol has devoted her professional life to celebrating and understanding children. In this beautiful, concise book she has gathered years of insight into child development and the nuts and bolts of effective parenting. I can't wait to share it with my own clients.

"This thin volume contains the distilled wisdom gleaned from Ms. Benchimol's years of celebrating, teaching and observing children. The author has a rare gift for helping parents reduce power struggles and cultivate loving, effective communication with their children. A welcome primer to parenting...

"The root cause of many parenting struggles is underestimating children's intelligence and not having the tools to help them emotionally self-regulate. This thin volume contains the distilled wisdom of the author's decades of teaching, writing, and celebrating children. It is a welcome primer to parenting that I will share with many of my own clients".

– Robert L. Wymss, MSW, LCSW

PEARLS FOR PARENTS' HAPPINESS

The Art of Parenting Through Inner Love

Brigitte Benchimol

Pearls for Parents' Happiness
The Art of Parenting Through Inner Love
Copyright © 2020 by Brigitte Benchimol

All rights reserved. No part of this book may be reproduced, distributed, or transmitted in any manner whatsoever, including information storage, or retrieval, photocopying, recording, and other electronic or mechanical methods in whole or in part (except for brief quotations in critical articles or reviews), without written permission from the author.

For information please contact:
Brigitte Benchimol
bbenchy@gmail.com

Other books from the author:
The award-winning children's book series
Jadyn and the Magic Bubble
including these three titles:
Jadyn and the Magic Bubble: Discovering India
Jadyn and the Magic Bubble: I Met Gandhi
Jadyn and the Magic Bubble: Kenya! Kenya!

Soft cover with black and white interior ISBN: 978-0-9830393-7-2
Hard cover with color interior ISBN: 978-0-9830393-8-9
E-Book ISBN: 978-0-9830393-9-6

Cover art by Brigitte Benchimol.
All inside art by Brigitte Benchimol.

Copyright © 2020 by Brigitte Benchimol

Published by B-Happy Press

Gratitude

To Troy, my soulmate, best partner I ever had, celebrating over eleven years of happiness and inspiration…and more to come.

To Marcel and Denyse, my loving parents always ready to help even from beyond.

To my sisters and brothers, Maguy, Katy, David and Robert, for being such a supportive family full of love and kindness.

To my nieces and nephews, Elisa, Haim, Daniel-Guy, Shira, Rémy, Ouriel, Oshrat, Fanny, Nicolas, Raphaële, and Jérémy, for being so loving and bringing so much laughter in my life. To all their equally amazing children.

To Deborah and her wonderful mojo group of ladies. Thank you for your support.

Pearls for Parents' Happiness

To my Director Sasha, for her balanced and joyful personality and all my team of dedicated teachers at Creative Mind Preschool. You are deeply appreciated.

To Mr. Genaro, thank you for being such a talented and ever-growing teacher and for our complicity in expanding our teaching horizons.

To my Creative Mind Preschool parents for entrusting all of us educators with their amazing children and trusting me with my guidance.

To all the children who came to my schools, thank you for teaching me so much, for shining your light and for your abundant love.

To all the parents in the world for this extraordinary adventure you live each day.

May the pearls of this book make you feel inspired, creative and happy.

Preface: An Aha Moment

As I was in the middle of writing this book series, I participated in a weekend women's workshop in Southern California. Gathered at a colorful hotel, we were exploring how to reconnect with our mojo, our life force, our core Chi. Basically, how to live a harmonious life guided by the source within.

As the presenter directed attendees to share their life challenges, it became apparent to me how hard it was for most of the women to recognize their value and to practice daily self-love.

Even amongst female entrepreneurs—who made up about eighty percent of the group—the quantity of doubts, shame, complexes, and traumas expressed was astonishing.

I'd expected these successful women to be confident and baggage-free. But even though they'd

demonstrated incredible resilience in creating "Superwomen" careers, they still had doubts about whether they could be "Wonder Women"—without realizing that they already were.

I saw my own reflection in that, too.

Personal insecurities—instilled by how we're raised, along with societal expectations—are felt by men as well. The complexity of untangling past images of what was demanded of them and sometimes still is, undoubtedly affects how they see themselves in the world.

Both men and women must redefine themselves under a new paradigm. We all need to examine our roles and decide who we *want* to be versus complying with what we think we're supposed to be.

Understanding what we need to be happy and then pursuing a meaningful life must be done on both an individual basis and a couple's basis—not a trivial task! But becoming aware of the challenge is an amazing start.

Having owned preschools for over two decades, I have focused my life on early childhood education, teacher and parent education. I've also focused on

Preface

my own personal and professional development. For me, the three are inseparable. I get tremendous fulfillment from helping and teaching others, paired with consistently studying anything that fascinates me—for example, neuroscience.

During the workshop, I couldn't help but reflect on the impact these women's self-image and self-appreciation—or lack thereof—had not only on their own well-being but also on that of their daughters, the future women of the world, and their sons.

My mind went to the classic airplane "oxygen mask" metaphor: During an emergency, when the masks drop down, parents are directed to put on their own first, before trying to help their children. I realized this valuable analogy applies to all aspects of parenting, and that's when the necessary focus for the book became clear to me. Thus, appeared the title for the first section: "All About Me."

Children are taught not only through words. Parents are the role models and *gods* of their child's life. Big Baby is always watching with adoring eyes, emulating your being, your feelings, your actions, and your ease in life.

Pearls for Parents' Happiness

So it really *is* all about you.

Therefore, taking care of yourself is the best gift you can give to your child.

PEARLS FOR PARENTS' HAPPINESS

The Art of Parenting Through Inner Love

Table of Contents

Chapter 1: All About Me

1. I AM: Celebrate Your Inner Beauty 4
2. Start Your Day with Inner Peace 5
3. Be Courteous 6
4. Share Your Passions 7
5. Collect Coping Tools 8
6. Have Fun! (Alone, and with Your Partner or Posse). 9
7. Change Your Words to Change Your Outlook . 10
8. Be the TOP Model. 11
9. Replenish the Water Within! 12
10. Ask and You Will Receive 13
11. Propose Solutions to Problems Promptly . . . 14
12. Sleep: Strive for Quality and Quantity. 15
13. Fall in Love with the Beautiful Brain 17
14. See Life Through the Eyes of Your Child . . . 18
15. Travel with Tiny Essentials 19

Pearls for Parents' Happiness

16.	Keep or Trade Traditions	21
17.	Carry Your Love Notes	22
18.	Express Yourself Authentically	23
19.	Update Your Inner Version	24
20.	Enjoy a Rejuvenation-Vacation	25
21.	Be a Lifesaver	26
22.	Practice Self-Love	27
23.	Reflect: Am I Helping or Am I Hurting?	28
24.	Beware of Alcohol's Effect on Your Brain	29
25.	Find Your Tribe	30
26.	Forgive for You	31
27.	Ask Yourself: "Do I Love My Life?"	32

Chapter 2: Boundaries

1.	Be a Parent, Not a Buddy	40
2.	Mindfully Manage Car Tantrums	41
3.	Offer Freedom Within the Frame	42
4.	Trust Your Child to Solve Problems	43
5.	Prioritize Safety and Security	44
6.	Choose Results over Excuses	45
7.	Keep Your Cool and Keep Your Boundaries	46
8.	Let Your Child Free-Play	47
9.	Show Respect to Earn Respect	48
10.	Mind Your Moods Because Your Moods Matter	49

Table of Contents

11.	Take a Family Screen-Fast.	50
12.	Stop Multitasking	51
13.	Peacefully Address Anger, Frustration, and Tantrums	52
14.	Limit Media Exposure (especially the bad news!)	53
15.	Demand Kindness.	54
16.	Create Consistency with Habits and Rituals.	55
17.	Apply the Four Agreements.	56
18.	Build Family Time Through Mealtime.	57
19.	Create a Healthy Relationship with Food	58
20.	Change Behavior Through Logical Consequences.	59
21.	Include Your Child in Daily Chores	61
22.	Reinforce Real Values.	62
23.	Create a Peace Space	63
24.	Disconnect from the Drama Triangle	64
25.	Monitor Your Mentality	65
26.	Counter-Balance Negative Thoughts	66
27.	Encourage Creative Clothing Choices	67
28.	Set Bold and Beautiful Boundaries	68

Chapter 3: Communication

1.	Choose the Compliment Cure	75
2.	Pick Your Words like Flowers	76

Pearls for Parents' Happiness

3.	Question Without Prejudice.	77
4.	Use High Vocabulary	78
5.	Argue with Love and Reach Resolution	79
6.	Communicate Clearly and Concisely	81
7.	Make Tedious Tasks Tender.	82
8.	Ask Genuine Questions	83
9.	Listen with Your Whole Being.	84
10.	Hold Firm to Trust, Truth, and Honesty.	85
11.	Keep It Simple and Straight.	86
12.	Turn to Children's Books for Support	88
13.	Express Disagreement with the Behavior—Not the Person	89
14.	Stimulate Active Listening	90
15.	Practice Positive Reinforcement	91
16.	Embrace Empathy.	92
17.	Communicate with Patience	93
18.	Show Your Love, Affection, and Tenderness	94
19.	Laugh with Love	95
20.	Ride the Ups and Downs	96
21.	Send Clear Messages	97
22.	Communicate Without Shame or Blame	98
23.	Hug, Cuddle, and Snuggle.	99
24.	Be Kind.	100
25.	Parents: United You'll Succeed!	101
26.	Cultivate Gratitude	102

Table of Contents

Chapter 4: Consciousness

1. Adopt a Mindful Mindset about Money 108
2. Appreciate Being Alive 110
3. Practice Positivity with Persistence. 111
4. Pursue Balance Passionately! 112
5. Be Fully In 113
6. Jump-Start a Fantastic Day 114
7. Open Your Mind. 115
8. Absorb the Beautiful Energy of Mother Earth. 116
9. Select Brain-Friendly Music. 117
10. Instill a Love of Animals 118
11. Teach Sustainability as a Lifestyle 119
12. Shop at Farmers Markets 120
13. Include Your Child in Meditation and Yoga . .121
14. Use Essential Oils as Preventative Medicine .122
15. Pay Attention to Energies. 123
16. Be a Human Being, Not a Human Doing! . . .124
17. Appreciate Food Delights 125
18. Help Your Child Welcome a Sibling 126
19. Promote Happiness as a Life Choice 128
20. Create a Caring Connection. 129
21. Embrace Big Dreams 130
22. Make a Difference in the World 131
23. Honor Your Relationship 132

Pearls for Parents' Happiness

24.	Adopt a Growth Mindset	.133
25.	Be Resilient, Show Resilience, Teach Resilience	.134
26.	Develop Mindful Tools	.135
27.	Journal for Self-Growth	.136

Chapter 5: Let It Grow

1.	Accept Your Child as Your Teacher	.142
2.	Study Your Child like an Anthropologist	.143
3.	Give Your Child Space to Evolve	.144
4.	Teach with Joy	.145
5.	Encourage Experimentation	.146
6.	Sloooow Down	.147
7.	Embrace Your Child's Personality	.148
8.	Treat Playtime as Precious Time	.149
9.	Encourage Your Child	.150
10.	Savor Each Moment like a Special Treat	.151
11.	Be Open to Your Child Remembering a Past Life	.152
12.	Encourage Discovery Through Reading	.153
13.	Promote Learning as a Fun Activity	.154
14.	Reach Out for Help	.155
15.	During an Emotional Roller Coaster Ride, Hold on Tight	.156
16.	Seek Out Resources	.157

Table of Contents

17.	Be Sensitive to Your Child's Fears	158
18.	Communicate with Your Preschool	159
19.	Handle Disagreements Respectfully.	160
20.	Get the School's Perspective	.161
21.	Pick Proudly Your Preschool Partner	.162
22.	Prepare for Preschool like a Pro	163
23.	Choose a School or Preschool that Matches Your Value System.	165
24.	Be Part of a Village	166
25.	Be Diligent about Hand-Washing	167
26.	Talk about Body, Privacy, and Sex.	168
27.	Prepare Properly for Potty-Pooping	169
28.	Encourage Friendships of Substance	170

Chapter 1
All About Me

Introduction

"Be the change you want to see in this world."

—Gandhi

All the major thinkers and life-changers in the world have said it: Everything starts with ourselves. So in order for our children to thrive, we must flourish first. Yet, all too rarely are parents advised to focus on self-love and to take time for their personal relationships.

Yet, if we want to be the best parents we can be, we must understand that when we, the adults around our children, grow healthy—emotionally, mentally, physically, and spiritually—they will too.

Pearls for Parents' Happiness

All the keys to happiness in this book were carefully selected from witnessing what makes parents blossom. One necessary ingredient is finding a balance between time for yourself, time for your relationship with your partner, time for your child, and, of course, time for your work. In that order, preferably, so you don't have any regrets twenty years from now.

Parenting is not a science; it's an art. While it may come more naturally to certain people, we all can master it if we want to. And parenting with joy doesn't require any extra effort; in fact, the job is easier when we use the right tools and philosophy.

To enter the realm of blissful parenting, we need to question and expand ourselves. We need to grow into the role. Taking this journey with a mindset toward growth rather than a fixed viewpoint makes us better parents and educators.

And we may need help—which is fine because there's plenty available, starting here. This book's goal is to provide keys to the doors of a happier and more fulfilling parenthood experience.

All About Me

And the great news? You are not alone. They say "it takes a village," but many of us don't realize that a village is all around us. We are surrounded by valuable resources. Family, friends, and schools can provide excellent support.

Ask and you shall receive!

It is crucial to develop a nurturing, loving, and positive support system. Just like children, we all need our daily dose of socialization and hugs!

And we are all on the same amazing mission to raise the next generation of amazing human beings.

So just remember: It's all about you!

Happy reading for easy breakthroughs!

~ 1 ~

I AM: Celebrate Your Inner Beauty

You are amazing and you need to own it! Write on a piece of paper the statement "I am..." with as many positive adjectives as you can think of about yourself: *I am kind, I am loving, I am amazing, I am gentle, I am courageous, I am vibrant...*

Write as many "I am" statements as you can for three minutes. Add to your list from time to time, and read it at least twice a month.

~ 2 ~

Start Your Day with Inner Peace

Read or listen to *Stillness Speaks* by Eckhart Tolle on your way to work in the morning—it's a great way to start your day. If your child is in the car with you, she will benefit from it as well.

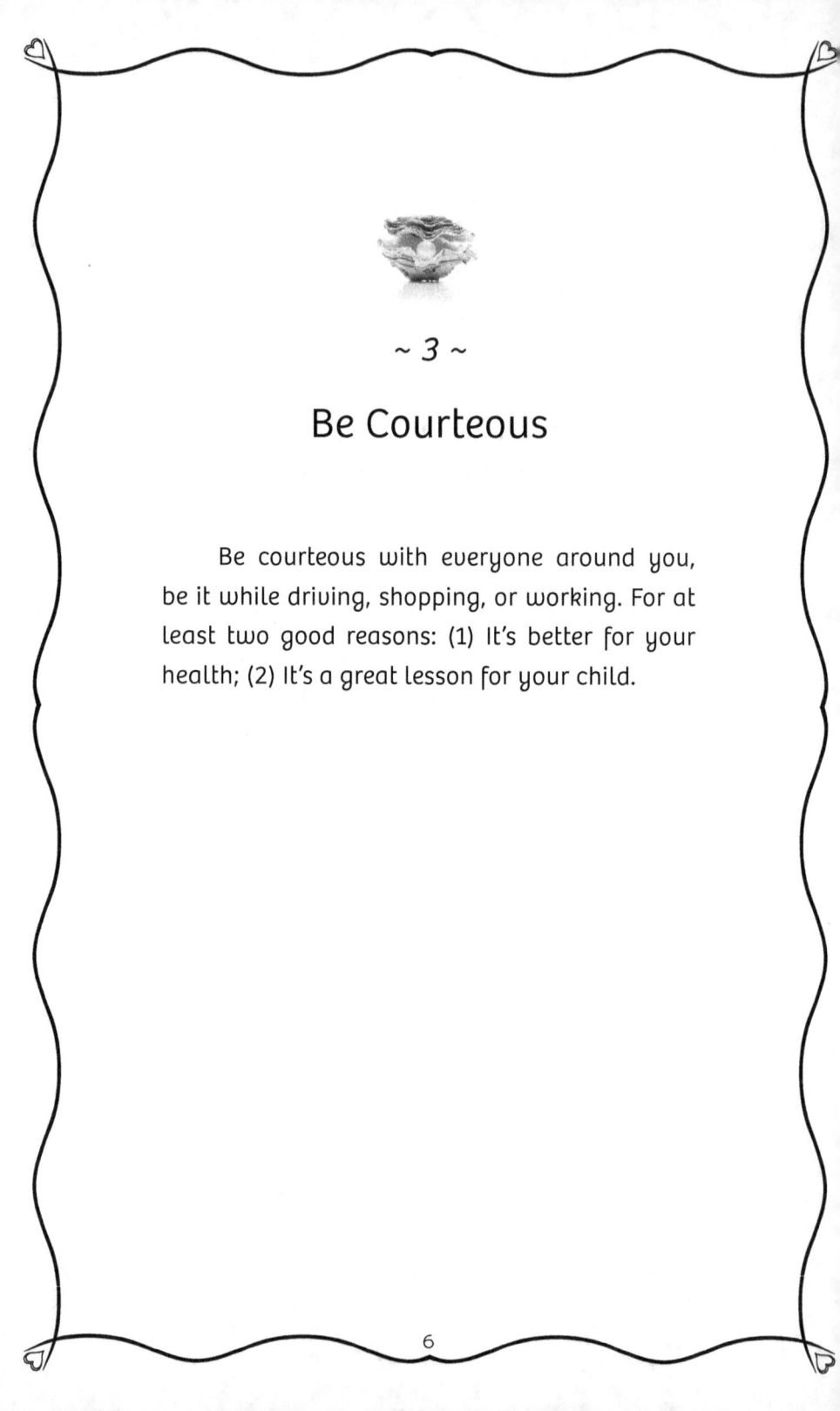

~ 3 ~

Be Courteous

Be courteous with everyone around you, be it while driving, shopping, or working. For at least two good reasons: (1) It's better for your health; (2) It's a great lesson for your child.

~ 4 ~

Share Your Passions

No need to give up the things you love when you have children—especially if you can integrate the whole family into the activity. If you love swimming, photography, hiking, or chess, do it and share it with your child and partner. Enthusiasm, joy, and passion are contagious.

~ 5 ~

Collect Coping Tools

Take time to learn a variety of coping mechanisms, such as deep breathing, changing your thoughts to change your moods, or smelling essential oils. Teach these strategies to your child, as well. This allows you both to face life challenges with healthy habits and resilience.

As challenging as it is, be diligent in using temper-cooling techniques when your child is testing you. Take three long breaths and then slowly address the issue. Do your very best to respond thoughtfully instead of reacting from a less conscious place.

~ 6 ~

Have Fun! (Alone, and with Your Partner or Posse)

PLAY, PLAY, PLAY! Yes, you, parents!

Make time to play and enjoy life as a couple. If you don't have a partner, pick your most fun friend or family member.

Dedicate time for having fun by yourself, too. And dedicate time for having fun with your family.

Playing even a few minutes daily will recharge your energy.

~ 7 ~

Change Your Words to Change Your Outlook

Replace "should" with "could." For example: "I *could* organize my closet this weekend."

"Could" opens possibilities while "should" creates a sense of an obligation or burden.

~ 8 ~

Be the TOP Model

You are the role model and the top model, so your child will often act as your mirror. Demonstrate what respectful behaviors are by speaking with kind and respectful words and behaving respectfully towards others.

Children emulate our actions, so we can't just tell them "Do what I say but not what I do" because it doesn't work. We learn through experience and especially through watching our parents and siblings, aka our Heroes!

~ 9 ~

Replenish the Water Within!

We are 70 percent water and children are even more! Therefore it's crucial to choose water as your family's main source of hydration.

If anyone gets bored from time to time, add fresh basil leaves, fresh mint leaves, cucumber slices, strawberries, rose water, or orange blossom water. It's delicious and has no added sugar.

~ 10 ~

Ask and You Will Receive

Set intentions in order to manifest what you want.

Whatever your beliefs are—God, Goddess, Universe—ask for what you want rather than focusing on what you don't want or dislike. Our manifestation goes where our energy goes: they play together in parallel.

Our children are adept at freely imagining positive outcomes without fear or second-guessing. They show us how magical life is.

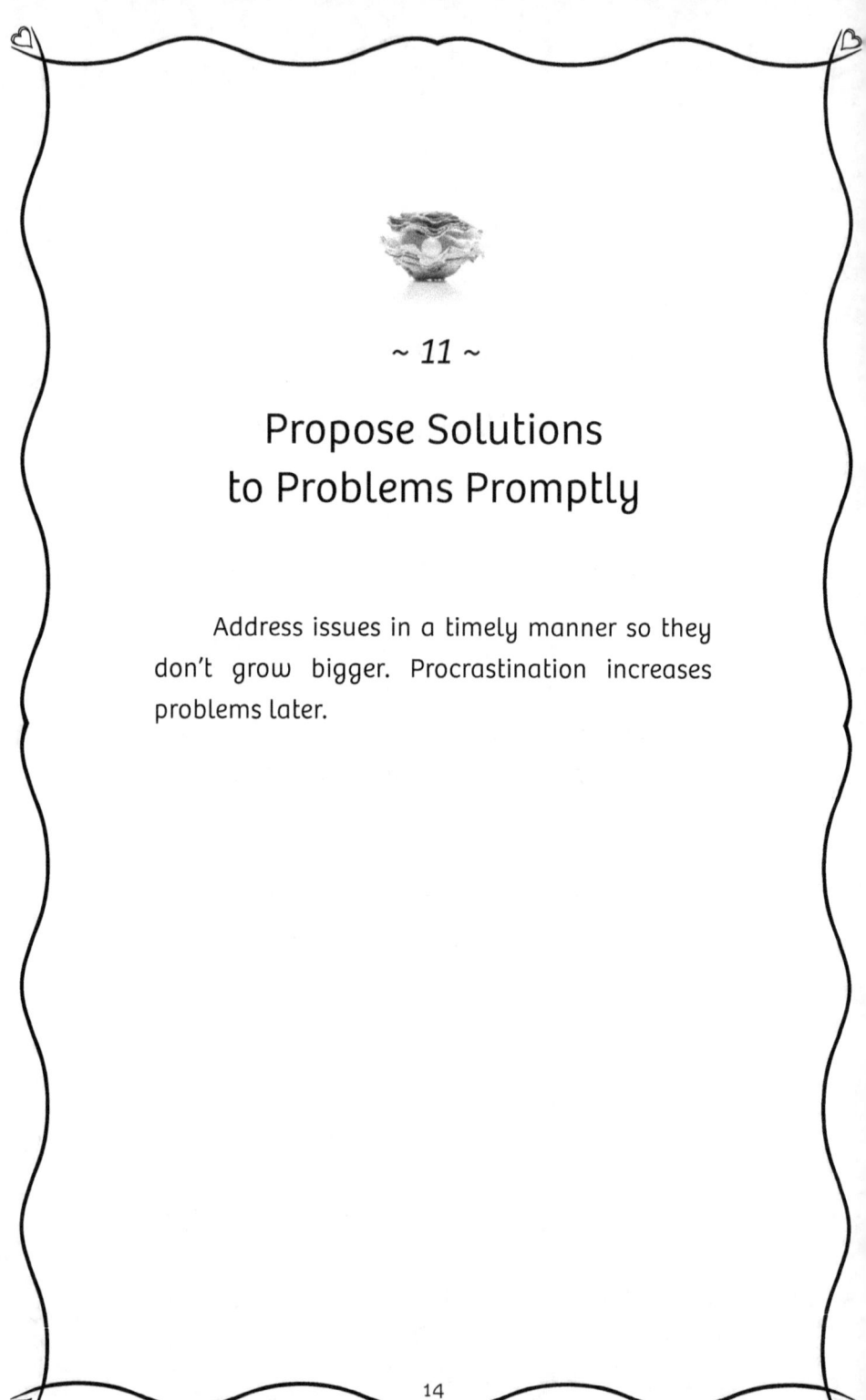

~ 11 ~

Propose Solutions to Problems Promptly

Address issues in a timely manner so they don't grow bigger. Procrastination increases problems later.

~ 12 ~

Sleep: Strive for Quality and Quantity

For adults and children alike, sleeping is an essential part of our mental and emotional well-being. Lack of sleep affects our moods and overall brain function, so consider sleep a much-needed shower for our brain.

Do your best to get at least seven to eight hours of good quality sleep per night. Children, depending on their age, need ten to twelve hours.

If your child resists going to bed, here's a trick of the trade. Tell your child: "I will grant you three wishes for the next fifteen minutes, and that will be it." Sample wishes can be:

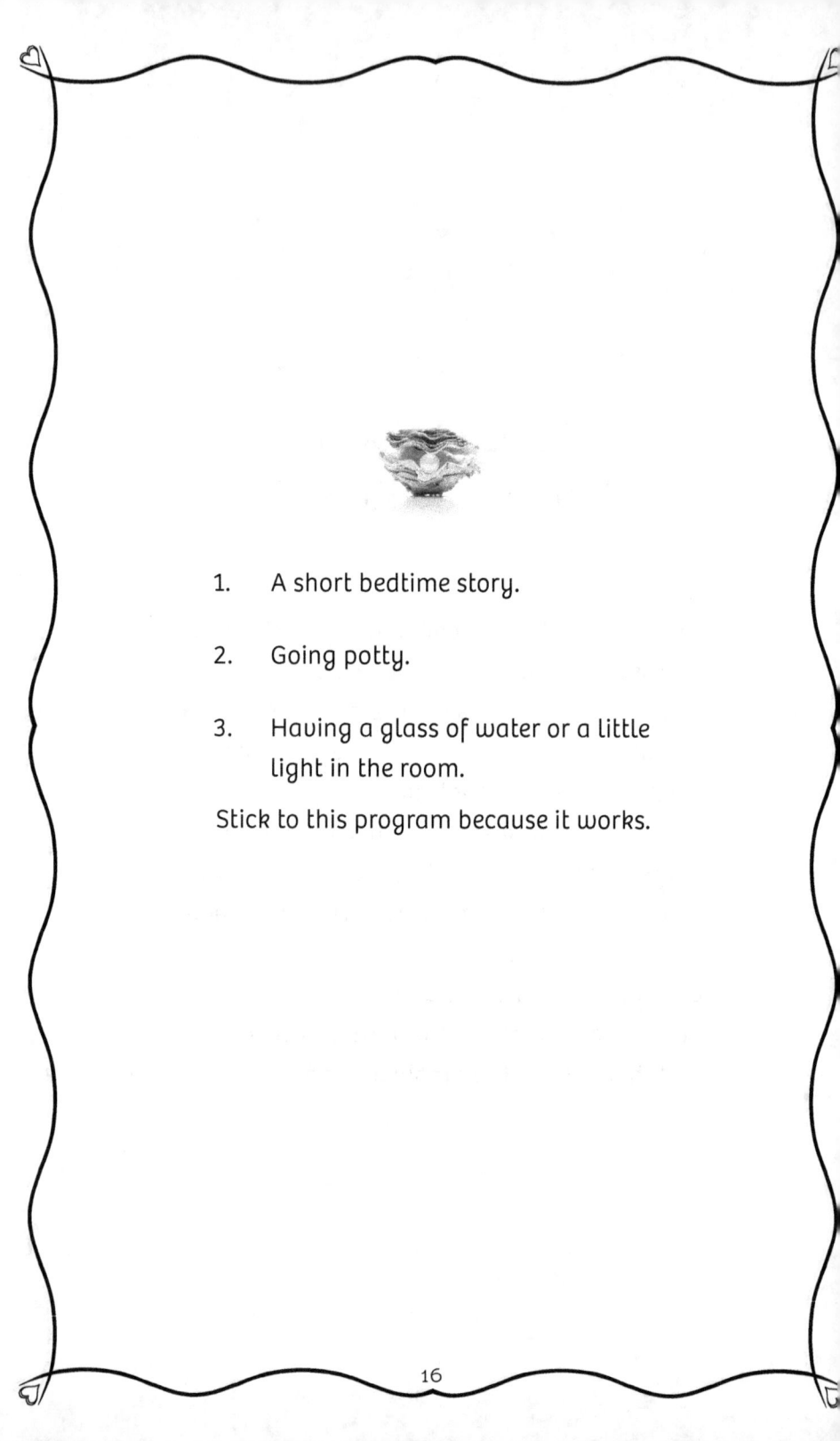

1. A short bedtime story.

2. Going potty.

3. Having a glass of water or a little light in the room.

Stick to this program because it works.

~ 13 ~
Fall in Love with the Beautiful Brain

Neuroscience is fascinating. Every day we are discovering a little more about the power of our brains and how to unleash our talents and gifts.

Learning about the brain will unravel a lot of mysteries of our human behaviors as children and adults.

~ 14 ~

See Life Through the Eyes of Your Child

Look at life through your child's eyes: It's so much fun! Witness how much children laugh in comparison to adults.

By seeing life in a true, simple, and innocent way, our children often hold the keys to happiness.

~ 15 ~

Travel with Tiny Essentials

Here are some items that will keep your child—and *you*—comfortable and safe on your next trip:

1. **EarPlanes:** For air travel, these pressure-regulating earplugs help reduce discomfort. It will save tremendous pain, especially if you or your child has a cold. They're great for the whole family!

2. **Motion sickness pressure-point bracelet:** Wonderful for the plane, the car, and especially your next boat ride!

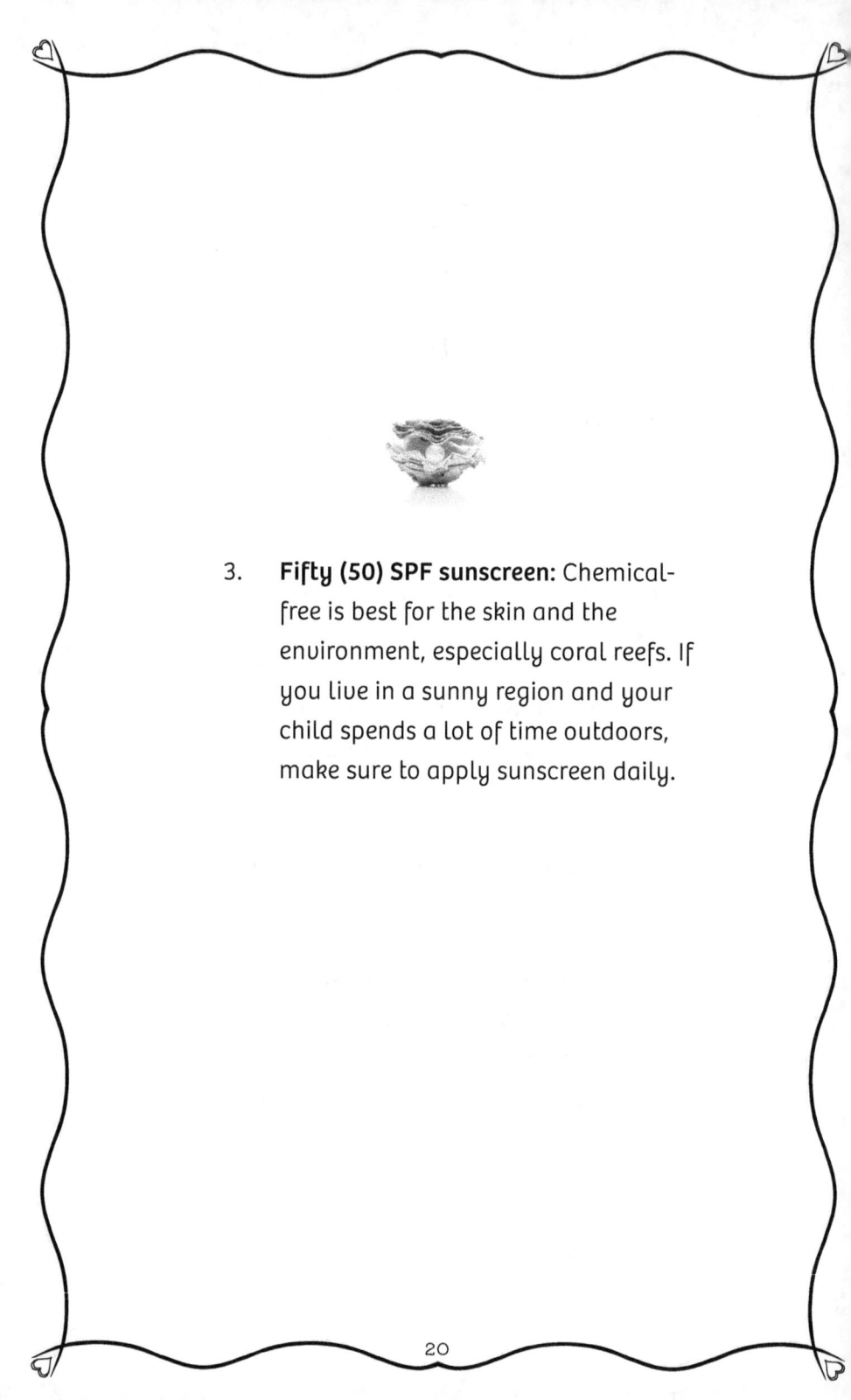

3. **Fifty (50) SPF sunscreen:** Chemical-free is best for the skin and the environment, especially coral reefs. If you live in a sunny region and your child spends a lot of time outdoors, make sure to apply sunscreen daily.

~ 16 ~

Keep or Trade Traditions

Question your belief system and traditions regularly, evaluating which ones still serve you in terms of personal and spiritual growth.

Even when things have been done for centuries, they may not necessarily be right for you and your family. If certain traditions or rituals don't make you happy, replace them with new ones that do.

~ 17 ~

Carry Your Love Notes

Keep at least three small love notes in your wallet from your favorite people. On rainy days when you're feeling down, read them to re-create the joy of when you first received them.

~ 18 ~

Express Yourself Authentically

Be Real: Say what you mean and mean what you say.

Be yourself, be consistent, and follow your intuition.

Don't say "yes" out of fear of being unloved, rejected, or confronted. Express how you feel and what you need.

If you use your word as your promise, you will be even more loved. Canceling at the last minute without extremely good reason creates anxiety and promotes flaky behavior in your child.

Be real, be truthful, be authentic.

~ 19 ~

Update Your Inner Version

What is the upgraded version of yourself—your 2.0 version? Your 3.0? Upgrade yourself regularly from the inside out.

For example, your new version could have the ability to forgive someone who hurt you; grudges are way too heavy to carry. Other upgrades could allow you to reach out for help or pursue something close to your heart you've been postponing for too long. Make the resolution, write it on a sticky note, give yourself a deadline, and celebrate yourself for doing it! See how much peace and happiness comes from installing your new self-updated version!

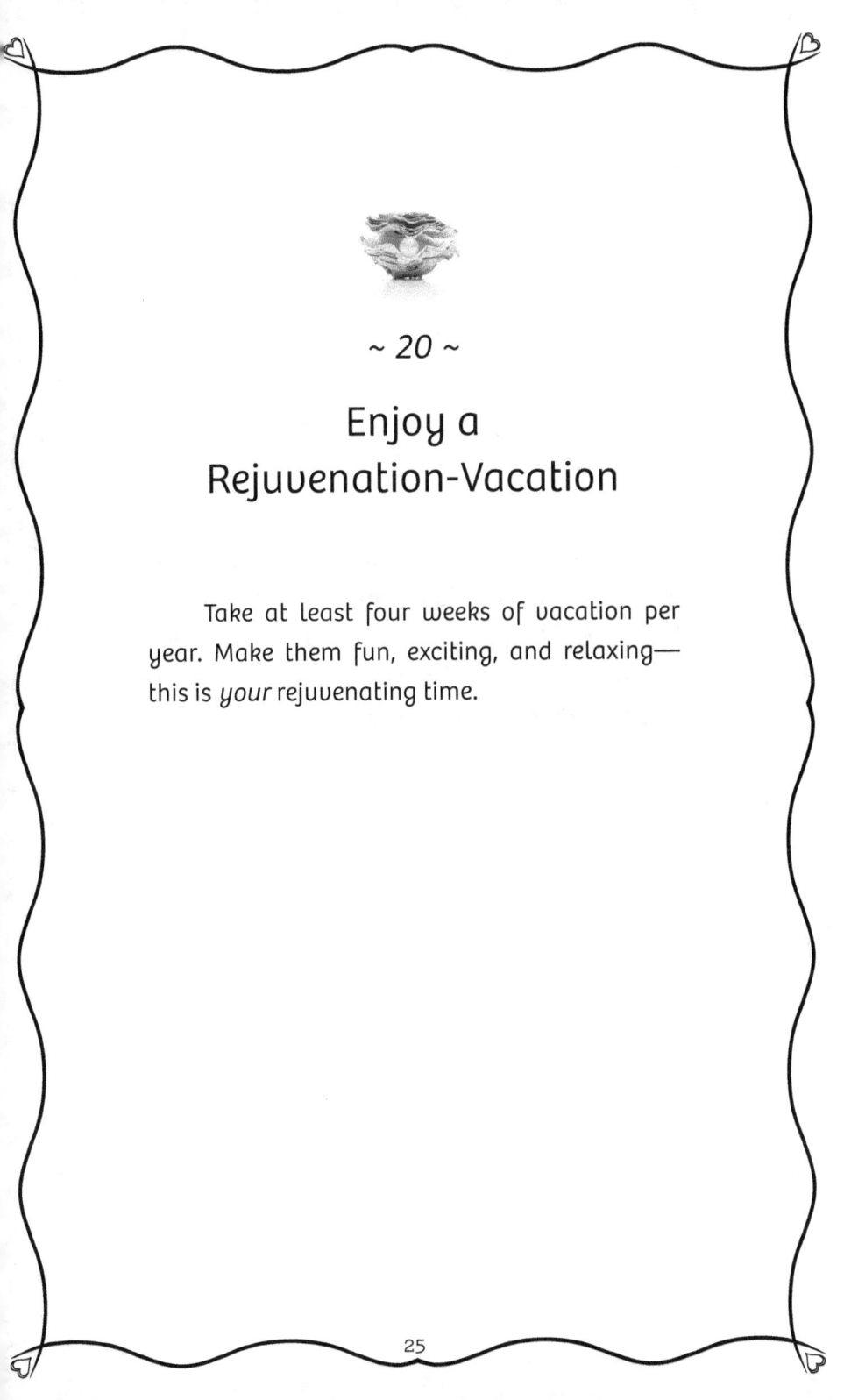

~ 20 ~

Enjoy a Rejuvenation-Vacation

Take at least four weeks of vacation per year. Make them fun, exciting, and relaxing—this is *your* rejuvenating time.

~ 21 ~

Be a Lifesaver

Take an in-person CPR and first-aid class every two years, so you can save your life and the lives of those around you. Certification courses are easy and are offered regularly by the National CPR Foundation and the Red Cross.

~ 22 ~

Practice Self-Love

For parents, teachers, and caregivers in general, it's essential to recharge ourselves since we give so much to others.

Show daily self-love by giving yourself attention and compliments daily. Allow yourself to be a receiver, not only a giver: Let others cherish you because they feel the same pleasure you feel when you give.

~ 23 ~

Reflect: Am I Helping or Am I Hurting?

Ask yourself often if you are helping yourself, your child, and your partner, or if you're hurting by not achieving the result you intended originally.

If it's the latter, just readjust course; when you change, everything changes around you.

~ 24 ~

Beware of Alcohol's Effect on Your Brain

Consuming even one glass of wine per day has been associated with Alzheimer's disease, according to Dr. Daniel Amen, aka Dr. Brain.

Developing healthy habits and healthy coping tools is essential to maintaining your quality of life.

~ 25 ~

Find Your Tribe

Join a group that makes you feel like part of something you love and contains like-minded people who are kind, positive, and uplifting.

~ 26 ~

Forgive for You

Show your child the peace of mind that comes from forgiveness.

~ 27 ~

Ask Yourself: "Do I Love My Life?"

You know the old proverb: "If Mama ain't happy, nobody is happy!" The reality is: If parents aren't happy, children won't be either.

And you deserve to be happy! Happiness is not only an energy we experience deeply but a state of consciousness in which we choose to live. A lot of joy comes from having a peaceful, drama-free life.

Ask yourself regularly: "Do I love my life? Is my life peaceful or chaotic? What changes do I need to make to craft the life I crave?"

Sometimes making tiny changes can shift the entire family dynamic. Keeping consistency and a daily schedule helps children feel in control of their lives and therefore more at ease.

Chapter 2
Boundaries

Introduction

Setting specific boundaries for children is like building guardrails along a mountain road: these boundaries make our children feel safe, guiding them through their winding journey.

Neuroscientists who study the brain and its impact on human behavior report convincing evidence that feeling safe is essential to a child's well-being and brain development.

I have witnessed the detrimental impact of parents who fail to develop boundaries with their children, and in many cases those children push their parents around, trying to see where they can find those boundaries.

Usually, the parents who get this treatment are the ones who regularly justify the child's behavior with constant excuses, such as: "he must be tired," "she might be hungry," "it's normal, children keep their composure all day at school and then relax with us and reserve their worst behavior for us parents when they come home from school."

Well, it is as you believe!

But let me emphasize an important fact: no, it's not "normal," nor is it an acceptable behavior. You can change it, and you and your child will be happier for it as a result.

Your child has the right to disagree with you when you stick with your boundaries. You are also teaching your child resilience. Resilience is this essential quality we all need to be happy in life: this acceptance of the actual situation we can't change—which may not be ideal—but is not so bad after all. The goal is for children to come to the final conclusion: "it's OK" or "I can handle it"—vs falling apart. The sooner children understand that sometimes they will not have the control of the situation, the better they are. They are building a strong foundation for a life which inevitably will confront them at times with disappointments

Boundaries

and rejections. Their attitude toward each situation will determine and shape the kind of life they will have as they mature.

Also, how you handle crises will show your child how it is "supposed" to be done: with ease or struggles – with Zen or drama.

Never forget that you, as parents, are the most important people in your children's lives.

Your crucial role is to make them feel safe. How is that accomplished?

Let's start with three primary "ingredients": Love, Mutual Respect, and Boundaries.

Then mix the ingredients with:

- Knowing when to say no and how to say it, with confidence, love, and kindness but not with apologetic mushiness!
- Being clear and consistent so your child knows what to expect.
- Making sense with those boundaries—which will also mean that life makes sense from your child's perspective.
- Giving your child a lot of freedom in other

areas such as self-expression, playing, having feelings, and exploring life.

You are giving a frame of reference—or a nest if you prefer—to your child, and within the frame your child will need to be free to explore without the constant input from an adult so she can develop a healthy sense of independence, of freedom, and therefore self-confidence.

The point of having boundaries in your life with your child is not to restrain but to expand her freedom.

Your child also needs to have her own boundaries respected.

She is not a mini-me, but her own person.

When she wants to do something on her own – if safe – let her do it as often as possible – respecting her space, skills, time and willingness to explore, without hovering, hurrying or showing "the best way" to do it.

Giving your child the heads up when you are leaving a place, a situation or a person at least five to ten minutes before transitioning is also being respectful of your child's boundaries and her need to finish what she is doing in a peaceful way.

Boundaries

Another child's boundary to respect is to listen without interrupting, putting words in her mouth, or correcting because you feel uncomfortable.

As parents and educators, we need to provide guidance, boundaries, and a safe environment for our children to be prepared for life.

Stopping at a red light is not optional. The sooner we know we have to respect rules to live in society, the better the brain makes the connection to do so.

So, don't be afraid to be the kind leader showing the way, enlightening the path – your child will love you even more for it.

When we are the adults in charge, they can be the children at play.

~ 1 ~

Be a Parent, Not a Buddy

Do you want to be loved first, or first respected? Good news: Your child will love you no matter what—he is born with unconditional love for you. You are the number one closest person to him.

Respect is the fertile soil that makes love flourish and grow healthily. While love is a given, respect we must earn through our actions and words. Being the parent in charge with clear boundaries sends the message to your child that you are the strong adult here to protect him.

~ 2 ~

Mindfully Manage Car Tantrums

Don't tolerate crying and screaming while driving—this type of distraction and emotional distress could endanger your safety.

If your child is having a temper tantrum, tell him it is stressful to you and making it difficult to concentrate. Inform him that if he doesn't stop, you will stop driving.

If he doesn't stop, park your car in a safe place, get out of the car, and take five deep, slow breaths. Watch your child calm down by your dramatic response.

Never leave your child unattended in the car for even one minute.

~ 3 ~

Offer Freedom Within the Frame

You are the adult in charge and therefore you make the rules, especially regarding safety.

Safety rules should be non-negotiable. Other rules need to be logical and reasonable, such as a set dinnertime or bedtime.

But within all these rules, your child needs to have freedom. Give your child real power by asking questions with a finite set of options. For example: "Do you want to go to the swimming pool today, or to the park?"

This freedom of choice is important not only for developing your child's decision-making skills but also for his happiness.

~ 4 ~

Trust Your Child to Solve Problems

An aha moment often comes after a struggle. If you want to see your child excited about finding a solution on her own, you must let her figure it out, being patient and supporting with the four super-words:

"YOU CAN DO IT!"

Give your child time and space to figure out answers and solutions without hovering over her or jumping in to "help." Her brain is developing—it's working and making connections at her own pace—and that needs to be respected. Your holding the space and time for her will send the message that she *can* do it all on her own.

Feeling capable of doing things by herself will boost her self-esteem and build a strong character foundation.

~ 5 ~

Prioritize Safety and Security

Bend down to your child's eye level, lock your eyes into hers, and place a gentle but firm hand on her shoulder or arm to indicate that this is top-priority direction. Then deliver a clear and uninterrupted message.

For example: "This is a dangerous street because it has a lot of cars. Sometimes bikes and scooters are on the sidewalk, too, which can be dangerous for us. Therefore, I expect you to hold my hand when we are outside, in the streets. Do you understand me?"

Do not add "Okay?" because you're not asking for her permission.

Make sure your tone of voice reflects the severity of the topic and that your child understands how important it is.

Let's be clear: This is life and death. So it needs to be addressed as such.

~ 6 ~

Choose Results over Excuses

Hold your child accountable to the boundaries you have set up.

If you regularly accept your child's reasons as to why he is not listening or being compliant, you are sending the message that your child's boundaries are not real nor firm and he can break them if he's too tired or too hungry or just because.

Be consistent and stick to your rules and verbal directives. This will give your child a sense of what is "normal" and acceptable in his life and what is not.

~ 7 ~

Keep Your Cool and Keep Your Boundaries

Your child may disagree with some of the boundaries you have set. Therefore, he may dramatically demonstrate his disagreement through various forms: screaming, crying, tantrums.

Your choice when this occurs is to give in to what she wants, or to wait it out until she stops and then talk about the issue.

The danger of giving in is that your child now knows how loud she has to complain to get what she wants. While giving in provides instant relief, the solution is temporary. And the reality is you will be handling a very difficult temperament for a very, very long time.

~ 8 ~

Let Your Child Free-Play

Overstimulation causes anxiety and boredom. To maintain proper balance, it's important for a child to have time to play on his own on a daily basis, without adult input. Free play will stimulate his imagination and creativity.

~ 9 ~

Show Respect to Earn Respect

That's right: You must respect your child to earn her respect.

Children are their own people. They are not our possessions nor are they mini-versions of ourselves. Children have commonalities with us and with each other, but more interestingly, they have fascinating differences that make them unique.

Showing respect to your child will teach her to respect you and the people around her.

~ 10 ~

Mind Your Moods Because Your Moods Matter

Pay attention to your moods so you can increase what makes you feel great and decrease what makes you uncomfortable, unhappy, or worse. This will make you more attuned to your child's moods as well.

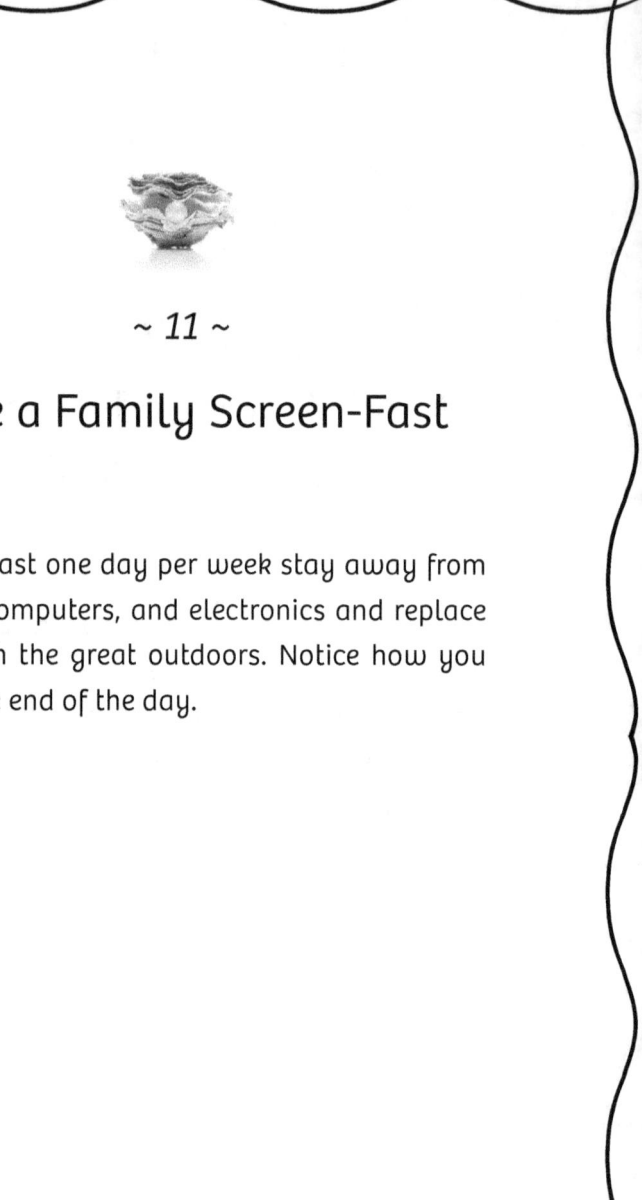

~ 11 ~

Take a Family Screen-Fast

At least one day per week stay away from phones, computers, and electronics and replace them with the great outdoors. Notice how you feel at the end of the day.

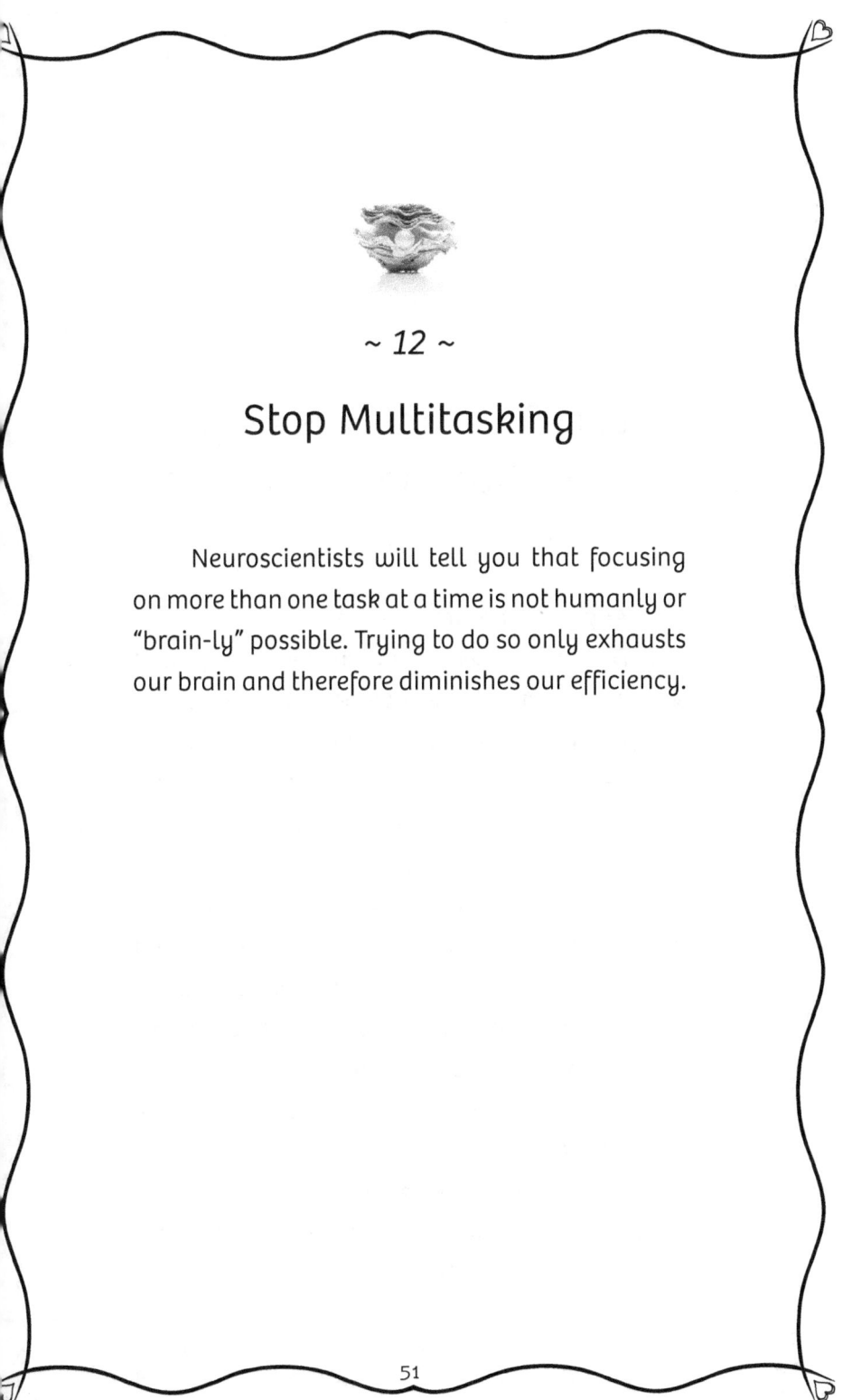

~ 12 ~

Stop Multitasking

Neuroscientists will tell you that focusing on more than one task at a time is not humanly or "brain-ly" possible. Trying to do so only exhausts our brain and therefore diminishes our efficiency.

~ 13 ~

Peacefully Address Anger, Frustration, and Tantrums

Anger is a natural emotion.

During your child's tantrum, just breathe and stay calm because it's his crisis, not yours. It's his way of expressing his disagreement, and it will pass.

Keep your cool and your boundaries. If you give in, your child will know that his behavior worked and will do it again.

Encourage him to express his anger or disagreement in a productive way. Give your child a soft pillow to punch, or a paper to write or draw on. Give your child a place to "find his peace" like a Peace Space, without showing judgment.

Give yourself a space to find your peace, too.

Correct your child if he is using a whiny voice to ask for something. For example: "Please ask me in a nice tone of voice instead of a whiny voice, because it hurts my ears."

~ 14 ~

Limit Media Exposure (especially the bad news!)

Carefully select what entertainment or news you expose your child too, as well as yourself.

News contains toxic information that can instill fear and a sense of despair or powerlessness. For children, it's ten times scarier.

~ 15 ~

Demand Kindness

If you don't hit your child, don't tolerate your child hitting you either—no justification and no excuses. Tell your child he can disagree with you by crying, punching a pillow, or going to a Peace Space but never ever by striking or biting you.

~ 16 ~

Create Consistency with Habits and Rituals

Implement good habits that bond the family. Avoid bad ones that separate—those ones are extremely hard to lose.

A good habit would be a ritual of going to the beach or the park with your child every weekend. A bad one would be for the family to stay home engaged in separate activities—one playing a video game and the other watching TV, for example.

Keep a regular and consistent schedule so your child knows what's next and feels more in control of life.

~ 17 ~

Apply the Four Agreements

Read and apply the "Four Agreements" by Don Miguel Ruiz:

1. Be Impeccable with Your Word.

2. Don't Take Anything Personally.

3. Don't Make Assumptions.

4. Always Do Your Best.

Explain these concepts to your child and—to ensure understanding and internalization—suggest she draw a picture representing each agreement.

~ 18 ~

Build Family Time Through Mealtime

It's great to instill in children that mealtime is a special social time with family or friends.

Make sure to share at least one family meal per day, sitting at the table for at least twenty minutes without TV or electronics. When you start this habit early on, even your two-year-old can sit for twenty minutes, even when done eating.

As often as possible, prepare healthy home-cooked food at regular hours. Safely include your child in meal preparation.

Avoid in-between eating except one snack in the morning and one in the afternoon.

~ 19 ~

Create a Healthy Relationship with Food

Associate food with healthy nourishment.
Avoid using food as reward or punishment. It may reinforce in your child's brain the relationship between feelings and the need for comfort food that could lead later on to obesity. If your child is crying and you feel the urge to give her something, offer a glass of water.

~ 20 ~

Change Behavior Through Logical Consequences

Every action and decision we make has its own natural, logical consequences. Use this fact in an intelligent way, avoiding fear or manipulation tactics.

Time-out, for example, has not much to do with understanding the consequences of our choices. It is easily perceived by a child as a punishment with humiliation attached.

On the other hand, if your child procrastinates in the evening when you ask her to clean up or get out of the bath, then her not getting to watch a show afterward because it's now bedtime is a direct consequence of her choice.

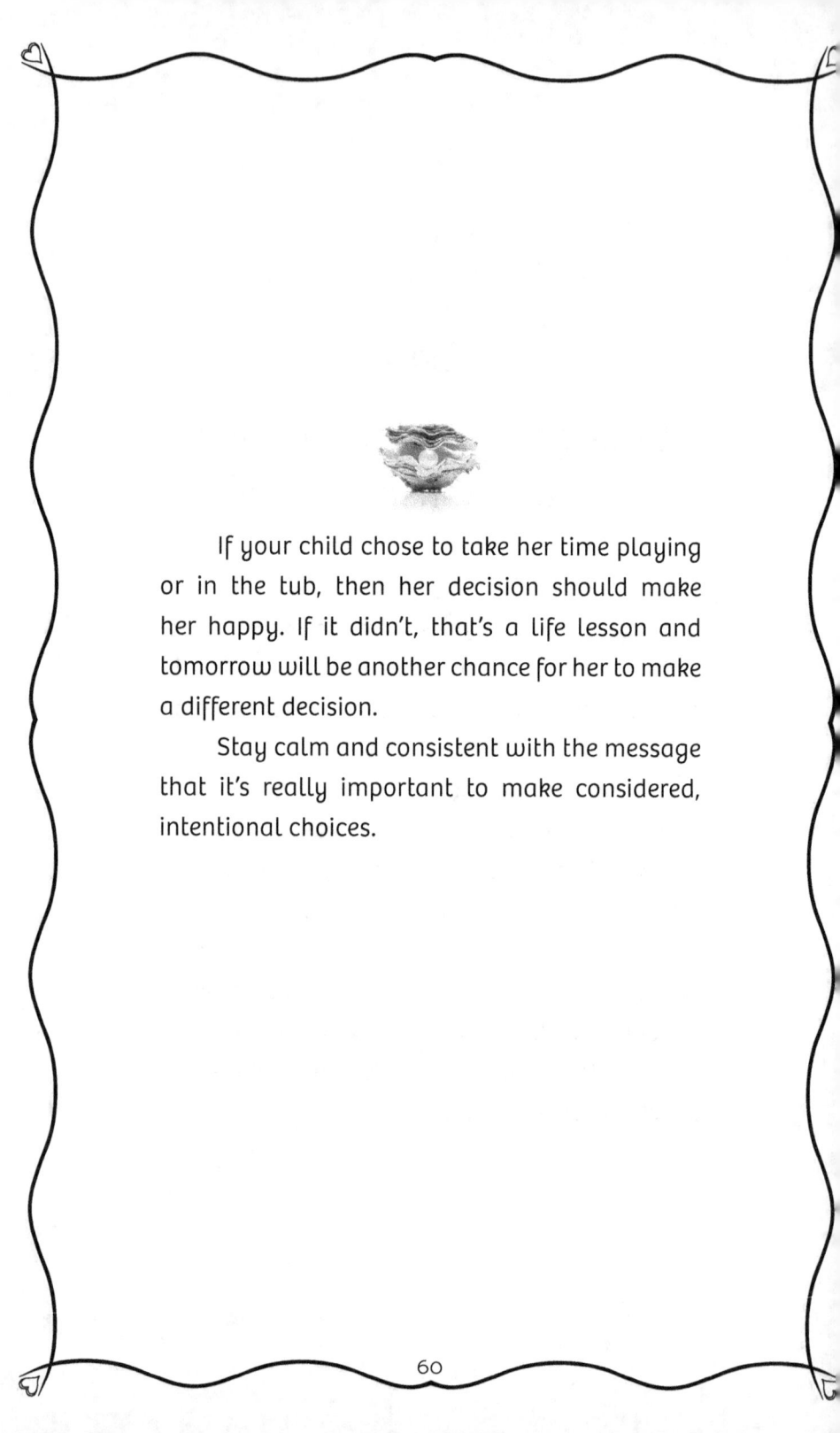

If your child chose to take her time playing or in the tub, then her decision should make her happy. If it didn't, that's a life lesson and tomorrow will be another chance for her to make a different decision.

Stay calm and consistent with the message that it's really important to make considered, intentional choices.

~ 21 ~

Include Your Child in Daily Chores

Keeping safety in mind, have your child participate in daily chores around the house, starting as young as two to three years old. Putting his plastic plate in the dishwasher is a good practice that is easy for a young toddler. You will teach your child early on what it takes to be part of a family or social structure with responsibilities and duties. It will make him feel included, too.

~ 22 ~

Reinforce Real Values

Talk to your child about your values and issues that are important to you. Here are two examples:

"When we meet people, we need to say hello. It is really important to me that you greet people every time you meet them because you are showing them respect."

"I expect you to talk to me with kindness. I don't yell at you and therefore you don't yell at me either."

~ 23 ~

Create a Peace Space

Create a Peace Space for your child where she can recover her peaceful mind. This can be a special chair or beanbag with a small toolbox that has inside a stress ball to squeeze, a plastic snow globe to gaze at, or a special plush toy to hug. Let your child decide how much time she needs to recover.

When your child is losing it, explain to her that the space is there for her to recover her peace. This technique is much more efficient than a time-out because it relies on self-soothing instead of outside shaming.

~ 24 ~

Disconnect from the Drama Triangle

The drama triangle consists of a victim, a persecutor, and a rescuer. No matter what part you play, if it doesn't make you happy, it is up to you to disconnect by giving up your role. Take responsibility for your actions, ask others to take responsibility for theirs, and set up new boundaries.

~ 25 ~

Monitor Your Mentality

Are your thoughts positive? Negative? Are you stuck on a loop?

If your thoughts don't make you happy, take three deep slow breaths and end each one with a long sigh. Try to remember three moments in your life that were pure joy and laughter, and build from that feeling. We are all energy, therefore your happiness or lack thereof is contagious and can pass to your child and beyond.

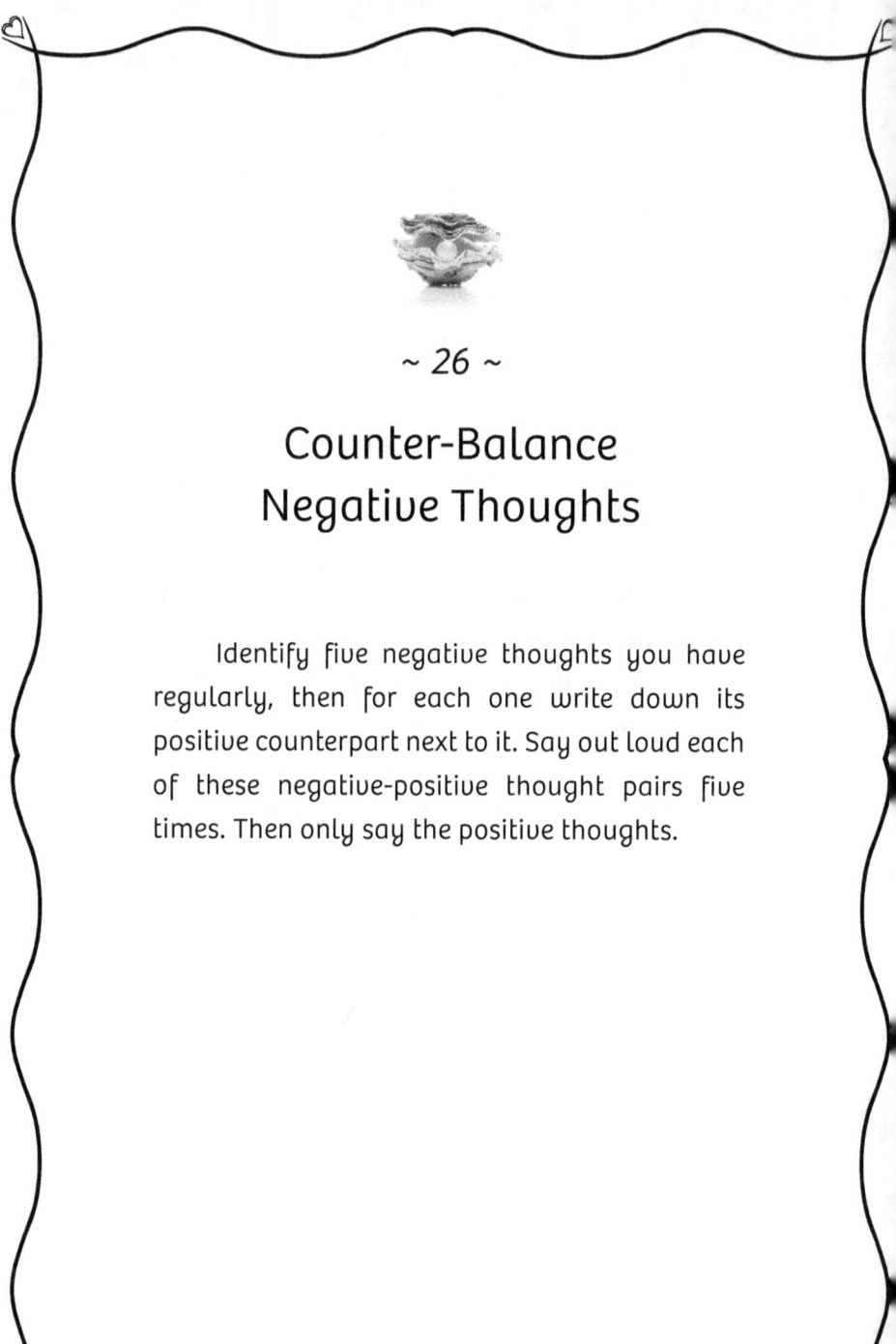

~ 26 ~

Counter-Balance Negative Thoughts

Identify five negative thoughts you have regularly, then for each one write down its positive counterpart next to it. Say out loud each of these negative-positive thought pairs five times. Then only say the positive thoughts.

~ 27 ~

Encourage Creative Clothing Choices

Let your child choose her own clothes if she asks to.

If her outfit doesn't match, it's all right. Your child needs to have some freedom of choice, expression, and creativity.

~ 28 ~

Set Bold and Beautiful Boundaries

Set clear limits for your child, informing her exactly what you expect. For example:

- "Be home no later than seven-thirty p.m., please."

- "I expect you to answer when I call your name."

- "I need you to set the table five minutes before dinner as I asked you to."

- "Please don't forget to clean the kitchen when you come home from school."

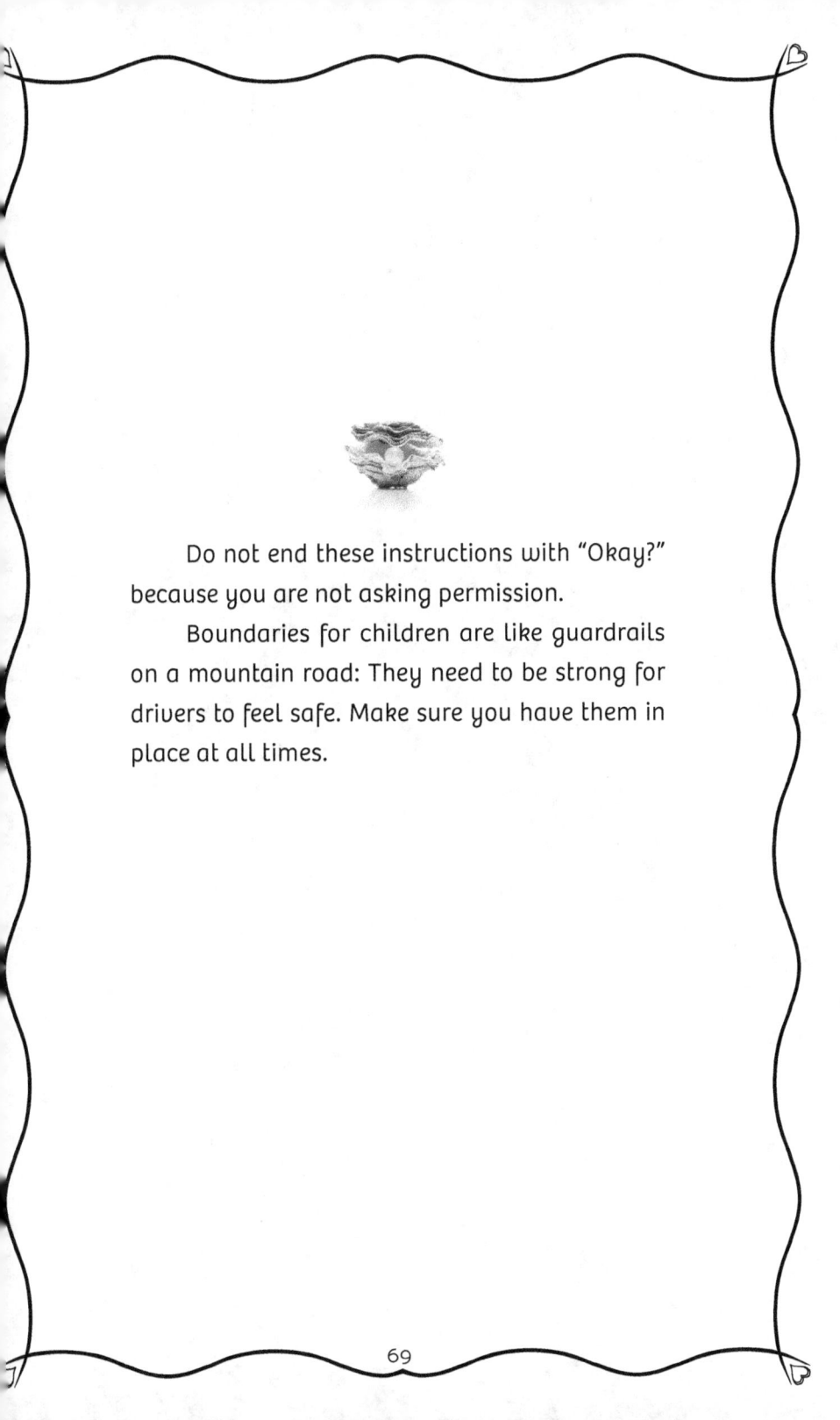

Do not end these instructions with "Okay?" because you are not asking permission.

Boundaries for children are like guardrails on a mountain road: They need to be strong for drivers to feel safe. Make sure you have them in place at all times.

Chapter 3
Communication

Introduction

Mindful communication is an essential tool for a family's harmony and happiness. We need to master it because it's the bonding agent that cements our relationship with others.

We all have experienced loving relationships in which poor communication has inflicted deep pain.

It is crucial to pay attention not only to what we say but also to how we say it—our intentions and our face and body expressions at that moment—because we communicate in so many different ways besides language: energy, thoughts, feelings, hugs, kisses, posture, eyes, and the tone of our voice. Children experience all of this and even more.

Pearls for Parents' Happiness

Listening with the whole body without interrupting or finishing sentences or even offering words is a crucial skill to acquire if we wish to become a great communicator. Listening in this way offers a chance for your child, for example, to take her/his time to formulate his/her ideas in a concise and clear way and will make him/her feel heard and therefore valued.

We all feel valued when we are truly heard. It's one important need that we all have: we want to be truly heard when we communicate. We all know that when someone or something is important, we listen.

And we all know that children hear every little thing even though they sometimes pretend not to!

I became aware near the beginning of my experience in the field of early childhood education that everything we say, we do, we don't say, and we don't do is a message to our children that they received loud and clear. Then they reflect back to us what they have received.

> "Like a trained surgeon who is careful where he cuts, parents, too, need to become skilled in the use of words. Because words are like knives. They

Communication

can inflict, if not physical, many painful emotional wounds".

Dr Haim G. Ginott,
School teacher, child psychologist,
psychotherapist, and parent educator

Today, we know so much more about children and about their understanding than our parents did. Our children are born to connect with us—how we do it will determine the adults they will become.

In order to communicate clearly and to achieve what we intend to, we first have to be aware of our own energy mood and feelings the moment we communicate with our children. Then, using selected words reflecting our mood or energy will help ensure an authentic communication. It will also send the message to your child that expressing our feelings through our words is safe and the way to go.

Connecting through our eyes to show love, compassion, pride, or disapproval is also a very effective way to communicate.

We know now that when parents are feeding their infant while looking and talking to their baby with

Pearls for Parents' Happiness

loving eyes, this child's brain will create more neuro connections and therefore develop faster, bigger, and better.

Loving words, hugs, consciousness, and authenticity are key to teaching our children how to be kind, to be real, and to live a meaningful life.

This chapter is full of keys, tips, and little life pearls to help you create daily habits of communicating with mindfulness, with authenticity, and with love.

Having a positive environment in all aspects of our lives—personal, partnerships, and work—is key to our happiness.

Communicating together is like a symphony orchestra with all of its musicians and different instruments playing this beautiful melody and creating music that makes us feel inspired.

We are the maestros of our lives. The type of music — or dissonance — we create, is our choice. The audience, our children, is listening.

~ 1 ~

Choose the Compliment Cure

Sincerely compliment your child and loved ones twice a day. This creates a rich soil in which to grow a meaningful and joyful family.

Ingredients of this fertilizer are well-chosen words that follow the word "You": "You are so... fun to live with"..."You are a compassionate and caring child."

This type of feedback reinforces confidence and self-esteem and helps define who a person is fundamentally.

One meaningful compliment mirroring your child's feelings is worth one hundred pre-fab "good job's." If each compliment doesn't sound meaningful and sincere, your child will tune out after a while.

~ 2 ~

Pick Your Words like Flowers

Words have energy, giving them the power to heal as well as the power to hurt. Using kind words toward ourselves and our children is essential to a happier life.

Positive and meaningful words—*wonderful, excellent, brilliant, amazing, fantastic, fabulous, extraordinary, divine, splendid, meaningful, conscious, aware, profound, purposeful, deep*—are beautiful music to your child's ears and to yours as well.

~ 3 ~

Question Without Prejudice

When asking a question, pose it neutrally. For example: "What happened?" instead of "What's wrong?"

An inquiry of facts instead of emotions helps everyone focus on a problem's possible solutions instead of having a discussion clouded by upset or blame.

~ 4 ~

Use High Vocabulary

Your child is brilliant. Raise the bar high and she will meet you there.

Use "high" vocabulary when talking to your child, as if conversing with Marie Curie, Albert Einstein, or Martin Luther King, Jr.—because your child is that smart! Talking baby-ish or very simply underestimates her inner intelligence.

Teaching children the words to fully express their feelings helps them avoid reducing hundreds of complex feelings to just happy or sad.

Apply logic and explain why you do what you do.

~ 5 ~

Argue with Love and Reach Resolution

Easy to say but hard to do, right?

Argue with love even when you are angry: To convey your point, say how you feel and what you need. Use the phrases "I feel" and "I need"; avoid starting any sentence with the word "you."

For example: "I feel ignored and sad when you don't call or text me to let me know you'll arrive an hour later than usual. If I know when you are working late, I won't expect you and won't worry if I can't reach you."

This will set a tone of compassion rather than defensiveness with your partner, your child, or anyone.

Don't use insults or harsh words—even if you feel you'd be making true statements at the time. Because you can't take these words back, and they'll be remembered for a really, really long time. Even a "sorry" later on won't delete cruel, painful words from the recipient's memory!

Do your very best to not argue with your partner in front of your child. If you do—it happens to the best parents—remember to show your child the resolution. Demonstrating that we can disagree and still love each other is a powerful life lesson.

"Mom and I disagreed about letting you watch TV until nine p.m. We talked about it and we decided that it will be better for you to go to bed at eight p.m., and we will read you a book for ten minutes instead. This will create a nice family time, and you will feel better in the morning because you will be more rested."

State this as a fact, not a question.

~ 6 ~
Communicate Clearly and Concisely

To set a path for an intentional and clear communication, tell your child precisely what behavior you expect. Say what you mean and mean what you say.

If you need your child to leave the house on schedule, use a timer to increase auditory cues and then give clear instructions: "We are leaving in ten minutes, so when you hear the timer bell, I need you to put your toys away immediately." There is no "Okay?" at the end because you are not asking a question or permission; you are making a statement.

However, it's a good idea to make eye contact to make sure you have been heard.

When the timer goes off, reiterate: "The timer went off. That means it's time to clean up and go now."

~ 7 ~

Make Tedious Tasks Tender

You can make a game of anything including tedious tasks because your child is always ready to play. For example, tell your child: "We have sixty seconds to put everything away" and then count down together. Another idea is to make up a song about what you're doing.

~ 8 ~

Ask Genuine Questions

Asking your child rhetorical or backhanded questions can instill fear or invite rebellion.

For example: "Do you want the big man to come get you if you don't go to sleep?" or "Do you want me to yell at you, or do you want to put on your PJs?" Your child may say: "None of the above! I just want to play!"

Instead say: "It's time for you to go to sleep now and have beautiful dreams" or "You, *Peter Pan*, need to put on your PJs pronto, please!"

Keep it straightforward and authentic!

~ 9 ~

Listen with Your Whole Being

When your child or your partner talks to you, listen intently with your whole body.

Seventy percent of our communication is nonverbal. We all know when someone is not really listening because they're preoccupied with something else.

Get down to your child's level, make eye contact, and listen carefully without interrupting or assuming.

~ 10 ~

Hold Firm to Trust, Truth, and Honesty

You are building a relationship with your child. It is essential for that relationship to be based on trust, truth, and honesty.

So if you have the blues and your child senses it and asks you how you feel, just answer honestly and explain the reasons as best you can.

~ 11 ~

Keep It Simple and Straight

If you don't know the answer to your child's question, it's all right to say: "I don't know but let's find out together." If you know the answer but are hesitant to verbalize it—for example, when your three-year-old asks you in the middle of the supermarket during holiday shopping: "Daddy, how do you make babies?"—you can respond: "I'll be glad to answer that question, but I need to give you a clear explanation, so I will tell you this evening, at home."

Make sure to stick to the time you said, because your child is counting on you.

Children are often underestimated. If your child asks a question, that usually means he is ready for the answer. So avoid making up a fantasy about the "stork" bringing babies.

Tell the truth without showing embarrassment or trying to confuse or evade by giving a complicated answer with unrealistic or strange words:

"How are babies made?"

"A little spermatozoid from Daddy goes inside Mommy's belly to meet a little egg and that becomes a baby."

Be precise, simple, and to the point.

~ 12 ~
Turn to Children's Books for Support

Buy children's books to help you with the big questions such as: "How do we make babies?" "Why do we have this new baby at home?" "Why are you and Daddy divorced?" "What is poop? "Why do we need bees?" "Why is Grandpa forgetting everything?"

Children's books exist on almost every topic, giving great explanations with vocabulary and stories that help children understand that the situations in question happen to other people, too, and help normalize their feelings.

For example, if your child has ADHD, or a sibling or friend with ADHD, try out *Baxter Turns Down His Buzz: A Story for Little Kids About ADHD*.

~ 13 ~

Express Disagreement with the Behavior— Not the Person

If your child is acting inappropriately, it's better to say "Your behavior is unacceptable" rather than "You are a bad girl." The latter statement labels who your child is intrinsically instead of disagreeing with her current actions.

It is essential for children to know that they are fundamentally good. When your child is having a rough day, shine the light on the specific time and behavior rather than her character.

One statement addresses something temporary and situational while the other indicates a more permanent character flaw.

~ 14 ~

Stimulate Active Listening

    Listen often with your child to *Peter and the Wolf* by Sergei Prokofiev.

    This story is an example of imagination, love, kindness, and bravery at its best. It provides a great active-listening practice and will uplift your mood.

    It's perfect while driving.

~ 15 ~

Practice Positive Reinforcement

Praise your child when directives are followed or efforts have been made. Positive reinforcement goes a long way with children, and also with adults.

For example: "You put your PJs on so fast and brushed your teeth like a champion. You are so independent with great listening ears and now super-clean teeth!"

Avoid downplaying or coloring the positive with some negative: "See? That was not so bad." "I always have to repeat things three times; why didn't you do it the first time?"

~ 16 ~

Embrace Empathy

Have compassion for your child's urges.

Thumb-sucking, for example, is an amazing built in soothing mechanism, making it a difficult habit to break. We adults have our own addictive oral habits that make us feel good: drinking alcohol, smoking, chewing tobacco or gum, sipping coffee, sucking on soft drinks with straws...

Make room for your child to cope with her own stress without inflicting further stress and humiliation.

~ 17 ~

Communicate with Patience

Explain the "why" of your directives: "If you suck your thumb your teeth may become crooked, so you may have to wear braces." Ultimately it is your child's choice on this specific topic. Shaming him will only result in poor self-esteem without stopping the habit.

Have the patience to explain things to your child in different ways, rather than repeating explanations the same way, and maybe louder!

Don't put words in your child's mouth. Give him time and space to process what you've said, and you will be surprised.

~ 18 ~

Show Your Love, Affection, and Tenderness

Show love through frequent hugs, kisses on the cheeks, and tender gestures. This is great for you and great for your child's developing brain, because it releases oxytocin, aka the feel-good hormone.

Use a gentle touch with your family as if you were caressing velvet. Be present and mindful when you do it.

~ 19 ~

Laugh with Love

We have all experienced how hurtful it is to be mocked or teased. Laughing with mindfulness means laughing at situations, animal antics, or even yourself—but not *at* your child or loved ones.

~ 20 ~

Ride the Ups and Downs

Children can go from pure delight to profound sadness in three seconds.

Communication is seventy percent non-verbal, so when you express your own joy or disapproval, it's important to match that emotion on your face and through your body language.

Sometimes a simple but intense look of disagreement suffices for a child to know she can't cross this boundary.

~ 21 ~

Send Clear Messages

If you are on your phone when you pick up your child from school, the message is loud and clear: My phone call or text is more important than you at this moment.

It's better to finish your conversation before entering the school and then giving your child undivided attention.

The same goes for your partner or anyone in your life. Make sure your priority goes to the people you care about most.

~ 22 ~

Communicate Without Shame or Blame

In order to get a desired outcome, clearly express how you feel and what you need.

Blaming and shaming will bring resentment instead of results.

~ 23 ~

Hug, Cuddle, and Snuggle

Oxytocin is a hormone released in the brain that calms and re-energizes the nervous system. This effect is activated each time we hug or cuddle someone. Make sure you give and receive plenty of both.

~ 24 ~

Be Kind

Treating yourself and others with dignity and compassion makes you feel great. Teach love and kindness through your actions, not only through words.

~ 25 ~

Parents: United You'll Succeed!

If you are co-parenting, you and your partner need to be a united team to raise your child and be happy together.

Take 30 to 60 minutes at least once a week for just you and your partner to talk about your feelings on raising your child, as well as your needs, your boundaries, and your reactions. Make it meaningful and special, with no TV, no music, and no electronic distractions. Give your undivided attention to the process.

Speak from your heart and listen from your heart to your partner. Begin statements with "I" rather than "You"": "I would really appreciate if you could consult me next time before taking our child to the ice cream parlor."

If you are co-parenting, you and your partner need to be a united team to raise your child and be happy together.

~ 26 ~

Cultivate Gratitude

Wake up daily thinking of three things you are grateful for. Share them with your child and partner, too.

Be specific and make them different every day:

"I am so grateful for all the love you show me."

"I am so grateful to have such an emotionally intelligent child."

"I am so grateful to have you as my partner because you are such a team player."

"I am grateful for all the energy I have, so I can give to myself and to others."

People who are grateful are happier and live longer.

Chapter 4
Consciousness

Introduction

Seeking to live a conscious life is like being a cosmic explorer.

Defining conscious parenting begins with first defining who we are as individual cosmic explorers.

Living consciously is living with eyes wide open with mindful responses versus eyes wide shut with "knee-jerk" reactions. For me living a conscious life means being ready to question everything I have been or I have done and being willing to change it if it doesn't serve me anymore. It's being aware of my impact in the world.

Is it easy to achieve? No, but it's essential to do

Pearls for Parents' Happiness

our best if we are to live a more meaningful, authentic and happier life.

As author and psychologist Dr. Shefali Tsabary would say:

"The quest for wholeness can never begin on the external level. It is always an inside job."

"When you parent, it's crucial you realize you aren't raising a mini me, but a spirit throbbing with its own signature. For this reason, it's important to separate who you are from who each of your children is."

Living in the here and now and being present without any distractions multitasking, or overstimulation and paring down to what's essential in life is a great first step to conscious parenting. Becoming aware of the impact our words and actions have on our children would be the second step, and a third step would be to stay real and authentic and true to ourselves.

The little pearls in this book will bring you closer to yourself and to the ones around you. It will get to the core of what is essential for living a blissful life.

When you use these tools for transformation, you will reap immediate benefits, and see how a small change can make such a big difference.

Consciousness

But one more important thought: we all know that time passes by quickly and children grow very fast, and you want to make sure that in ten years from now you'll say, "It went very fast but I enjoyed every moment of it, and I was right there by my child witnessing this beautiful soul 'expanding.'" You certainly don't want to repeat this all-too-common regret: "I wish I would have spent more time with my family."

Being aware of the fragility of life, of each moment at a time, and thinking regularly that we have no guarantee that we will be here tomorrow is not morbid. It's a wonderful reminder of how grateful we need to be for being alive every morning and getting another chance to make a difference in this world – through raising an amazing human, for example.

This time with each child is only happening once. Make every moment count and every experience meaningful and memorable so in ten, twenty, even thirty years from now it will still nourish your soul with pride and joy.

~ 1 ~

Adopt a Mindful Mindset about Money

1. Belief

Our beliefs about money often stem from our parents. Create a relationship of love, respect, and abundance with money so that becomes your child's experience as well.

2. Value

We only understand the value of money when we must work for it. Your child also will only learn the value of money through the experiences of earning, spending, and saving it.

Emphasize especially the amazing benefits of saving money.

3. Consumption

Less is more. Part of preparing our children for meaningful lives is by giving meaning to our purchases. Provide insight to your child as to what you buy for him and when.

Be consistent with your philosophy: If you are against war or don't want your child to be violent when he grows up, then don't ever buy a fighting toy like a plastic gun or a sword.

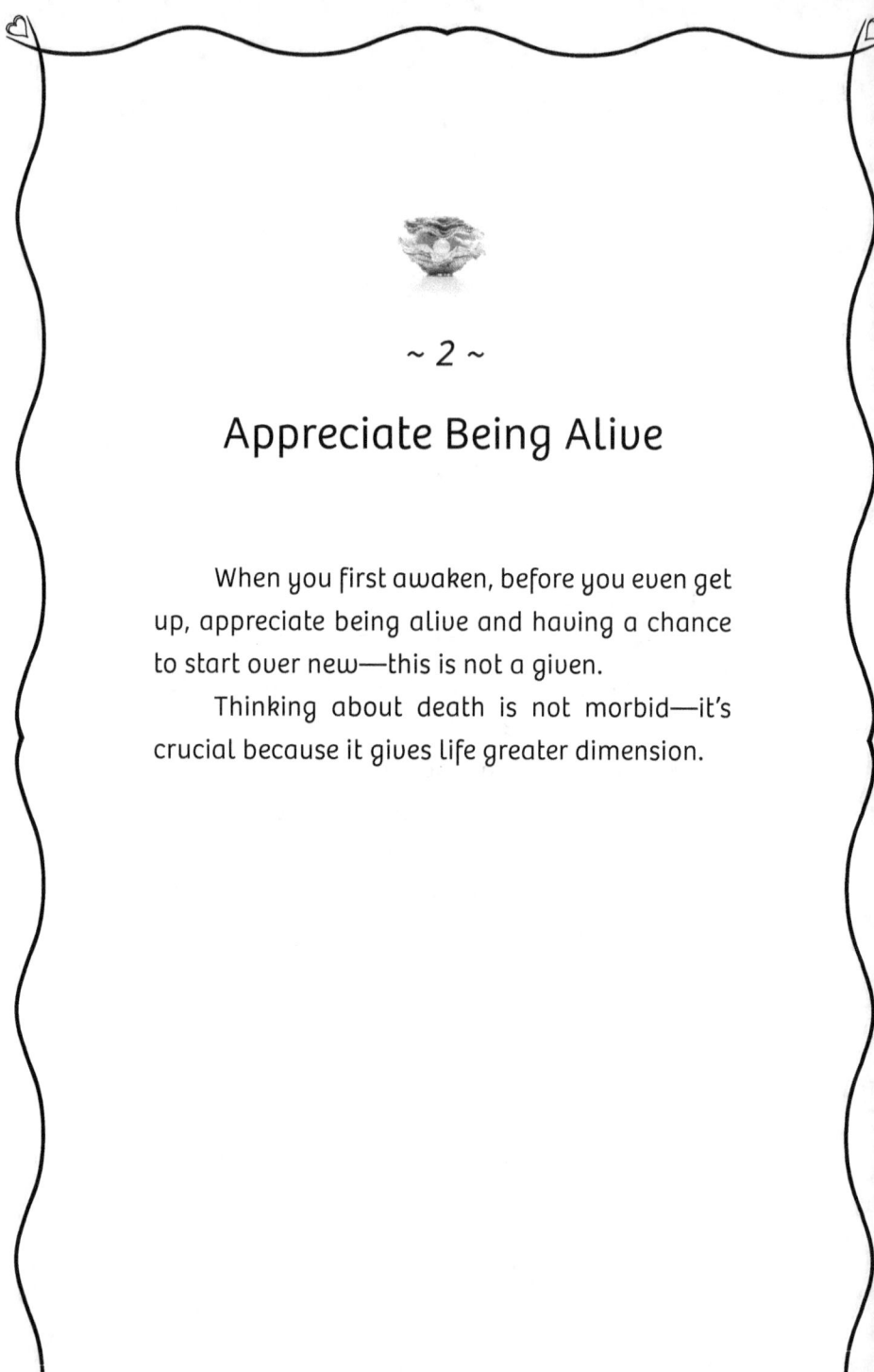

~ 2 ~

Appreciate Being Alive

When you first awaken, before you even get up, appreciate being alive and having a chance to start over new—this is not a given.

Thinking about death is not morbid—it's crucial because it gives life greater dimension.

~ 3 ~

Practice Positivity with Persistence

Cultivate positivity daily. Expect that things will work out.

When you get out of bed say out loud "It's going to be a fantastic day" and let the magic happen.

Surround yourself with positive and peaceful friends and family members who use kind and loving words. You will feel great and so will the people around you.

~ 4 ~

Pursue Balance Passionately!

Life out of balance can be stressful. If you sense you're working too much or your family is complaining about it, make changes quickly. If you find it too challenging, ask for help to make those changes.

We have help all around us all the time. We just need to ask and be ready to receive and adjust.

~ 5 ~

Be Fully In

Be fully present when you are with your partner or child. This means you are not engaged with your phone, computer, TV, or chores.

When you're on the phone or computer, your body is there but your mind and your emotional body are elsewhere. It's important to send the message to your family members that they are more important than whoever is texting you at the moment.

Greet your child every day after work/school with joy, gratefulness, and undivided attention. If you are on the phone, finish your conversation before your child arrives. Be totally available.

~ 6 ~

Jump-Start a Fantastic Day

Make each morning peaceful and meaningful. Get up early enough for you and your child to have fun, eat breakfast, and get dressed together. Sharing time together at a slower rhythm helps you start the day right.

~ 7 ~

Open Your Mind

Be open to new ideas, new people, new countries, or new knowledge—it's great for your brain and great for your child.

Attend the Conscious Life Expo once a year.

~ 8 ~

Absorb the Beautiful Energy of Mother Earth

Nature has such a powerful healing and loving energy. The great outdoors does wonders for the family.

Spend as much time as you can with your child outdoors, perhaps at the park. Walking or biking together for a whole day in the woods or near the ocean can be reenergizing and rejuvenating.

Go at least once a year to a family-friendly farm to pick your own fruits. This shows children where fruits come from and the importance of our trees and being connected to the earth.

~ 9 ~

Select Brain-Friendly Music

Observe your child's moods and reactions when you play certain music. We all know the power music has, and for children especially it can be extremely helpful or hurtful.

~ 10 ~

Instill a Love of Animals

Make sure your child has safe and regular contact with animals. This is a great way to teach kind and gentle hands. It also instills caring for others and respect for all living creatures.

~ 11 ~

Teach Sustainability as a Lifestyle

Save water, save paper, save food. Live by the motto: *Reduce, Re-use, Recycle.*

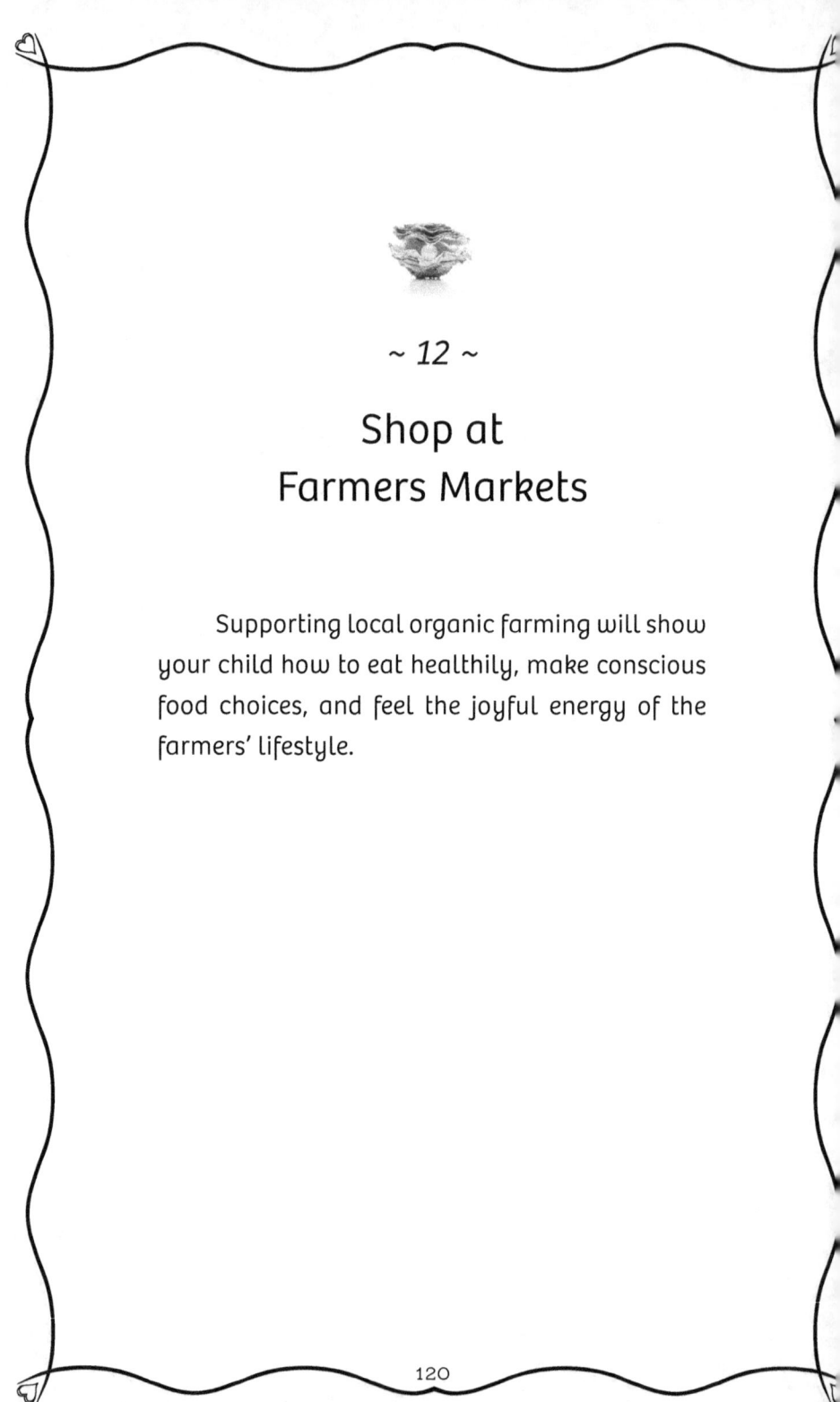

~ 12 ~

Shop at Farmers Markets

Supporting local organic farming will show your child how to eat healthily, make conscious food choices, and feel the joyful energy of the farmers' lifestyle.

~ 13 ~

Include Your Child in Meditation and Yoga

Doing meditation and yoga with children does wonders for their well-being. The younger they are when you start to practice with them, the easier and more beneficial it will be for them throughout their lives.

Make the activity fun and interesting so your child will look forward to this time together.

~ 14 ~

Use Essential Oils as Preventative Medicine

With the supervision of a professional, use essential oils for your own well-being and your family's.

From soothing yourself with lavender to strengthening your immune system with lemon, eucalyptus, and tea tree, essential oils serve as Mother Earth's gift to us.

Dispersing essential oil into the air with a diffuser makes you feel energized and healthy.

~ 15 ~

Pay Attention to Energies

We're made up entirely of energy.

Sometimes when we enter a room full of people or even an empty room, we feel something immediately. It's important to pay attention to how people or different spaces affect us, and follow our intuition.

Make sure you feel amazing entering your home and bedroom and that your child loves his bedroom. If not, burn some sage safely to clean the space energetically and make necessary changes until you feel better.

~ 16 ~

Be a Human Being, Not a Human Doing!

You don't need to keep your child busy or entertained every hour of every day. Allow your child to play on her own with minimal input or questioning from you. This is her creative time.

Also make time to enjoy life as a family. Plan unstructured activities together or just to relax together at home.

~ 17 ~

Appreciate Food Delights

Expose your child early on to a variety of foods, including dishes from different countries and cultures. Diversifying children's palates allows them to enjoy and appreciate everything for the rest of their lives.

Serve meals matter-of-factly without offering alternatives.

Include plenty of fresh fruits and vegetables. They are Mother Earth's treats for you and a great way to reduce our carbon footprint.

Don't worry about your child eating enough. According to well-known physicians and wellness experts Dr. Michael Roizen and Dr. Mehmet Oz, children know better than adults how much they need to eat.

~ 18 ~

Help Your Child Welcome a Sibling

Having a new baby is a radical change that your child may or may not love at the beginning.

Be patient and include your older child in raising his younger sibling by asking open questions like: "Why do you think the baby is crying?" and "What do you feel we should do?" This will make your older child feel important and included.

Prioritize spending alone-time with your older child. Your children's needs are very different, and your older child has gotten used to undivided attention. Make the time special and establish activities you do only with him while your other child is an infant.

Continue to reinforce both children's unique
gifts, without comparing siblings to one another.

~ 19 ~

Promote Happiness as a Life Choice

Instead of a time-out, yelling, or sending your child to the corner, explain to your child that every choice we make has consequences: positive ones make us happy and negative ones make us unhappy. The point is to teach your child to make decisions that will make her happy in the long run.

For example, if your child is writing on the table with markers after being told even once that she needs to write on paper only, a logical consequence would be to remove her markers and tell her to play with something else. If she screams and cries, this is the moment to explain that she made a choice that isn't making her happy and so tomorrow she may want to make a different choice.

The point is to prepare her to make the right life decisions for herself.

~ 20 ~

Create a Caring Connection

Ask your child neutral questions such as "How do you feel?" and "What are you thinking about?" and give her plenty of time and space to answer in her own words.

If you ask "How was your day at school?" your child may reply with a lot of stories or just a single word: "Good." If you get only a one-word answer, talk about your own day and most likely your child will soon find something to talk about in her day as well.

~ 21 ~

Embrace Big Dreams

Be supportive of your child's big ideas and dreams. Never underestimate her power to change the world.

~ 22 ~

Make a Difference in the World

Use activism to make a difference—either online or in person.

Create, support, and sign petitions to change laws and human circumstances through Care2 Petition, ThePetitionSite.com, or other platforms. You will be amazed at the impact 50,000 signatures can have.

~ 23 ~

Honor Your Relationship

Your relationship with your partner has three members: you, your partner, and the relationship. Nurture each entity individually and lovingly.

~ 24 ~

Adopt a Growth Mindset

Let go of a fixed mindset, which limits opportunities. Adopt instead a growth mindset, which opens a world of possibilities and unleashes your potential and creativity.

A fixed mindset takes you back to the same places you have been. A growth mindset leads you to discover new places, food, people, etc., and your brain creates new neural pathways with each new experience.

One mindset is restrictive while the other is expansive and limitless.

~ 25 ~

Be Resilient, Show Resilience, Teach Resilience

Resilience is the capacity to recover from anything. Resilience is not about the issue, the trauma, or the failures we are confronted with. It's about the ability to bounce back and move forward with more knowledge and wisdom.

We learn resilience through witnessing our parents being resilient. Dealing successfully with traumas and issues also builds resilience. Set an example your child can learn from.

~ 26 ~

Develop Mindful Tools

Mindfulness allows us to understand how our mind works and benefit from this awareness.

A mindful practice such as meditation helps you examine a situation from a distance and see it for what it is, allowing you to make choices.

Teach your child to use mindful tools starting at a young age.

~ 27 ~

Journal for Self-Growth

Create a journal for issues, problems, or traumas you are experiencing.

1. State the facts.

2. Record how the situation makes you feel.

3. Describe what you've learned from the experience.

4. Find something positive that came from it.

Notice how you feel before, during, and after this exercise.

Chapter 5
Let It Grow!

Introduction

This book was born as my teammates and I witnessed each day how parents responded to — and sometimes struggled with— the need to let their child grow. And we too, as early childhood educators, felt those same emotions as we prepared to let go of the children who graduated each year.

Let's face it: you can't stop it and neither can we! It's this inevitable cycle of growth and development happening before our eyes that reminds us that we too are growing older and our babies are becoming little children. It goes way too fast! No doubt.

But, there is a great sense of awe in watching the metamorphosis of our children opening up like sun-

Pearls for Parents' Happiness

flowers and becoming more vibrant, more secure, more independent, and even more loving as they experience this formidable expansion.

The beauty is that with each of your child's developmental stages comes joy and wonder. We discover new character traits, new skills, and new talents of this ever-growing human being.

This final chapter is entitled "Let It Grow!" and is written to help you gain some pearls of wisdom on how to maneuver such an emotional ride. You'll find practical tools to develop a support system to help make this fantastic journey of raising your child more conscious and more joyful. It will get you more prepared for the next stage to come.

The advice here will help keep you in the present moment to enjoy it and to savor it because the present moment is the only thing we have.

One of my favorite quotes is from Dorothy Canfield Fisher:

> "A mother is not a person to lean on, but a person to make leaning unnecessary."

Let It Grow!

The term *mother* is, of course, interchangeable with *father, teacher, or educator.* "Let It Grow!" is all about enjoying each moment of the discovery of this on-growing personality who we have the privilege to love, to witness, and to influence.

Savor this beautiful journey that's full of the love and joy of you raising your child.

Make this journey blissful and meaningful.

~ 1 ~

Accept Your Child as Your Teacher

Our children always know more than we think. Consider your child as your teacher.

Very often they tell us what they need through their behavior and sometimes with words. We just need to pay close attention and be willing to learn.

~ 2 ~

Study Your Child like an Anthropologist

Observe and study your child like an anthropologist—she is her own person and a fascinating one.

~ 3 ~

Give Your Child Space to Evolve

We are an evolving species, so give your child and your partner the opportunity to change.

We all remember too well teachers or family members telling us we couldn't do something, just because we got it wrong once or twice. Growth takes time, and we all have our own individual pace. In order to start walking, we had to fall several times and then we got it. This pattern applies to so many things in life.

~ 4 ~

Teach with Joy

You are your child's first teacher. Teach with joy, creativity, and enthusiasm. Be silly. Be yourself unedited! Make it fun and exciting, and then watch your child experiment his own way. You will be surprised.

~ 5 ~

Encourage Experimentation

Expand your family's horizons: expose your child early on to a variety of experiences and cultures. This includes trying different foods, going to ethnic festivals, traveling, and camping.

~ 6 ~

Sloooow Down

In urban areas especially, we tend to do too much and be more stressed because of it.

Children are slower than adults in many regards. So slow down...breathe...and patiently observe your child without doing or saying anything. Just watch and connect with her through your eyes. Such moments are precious.

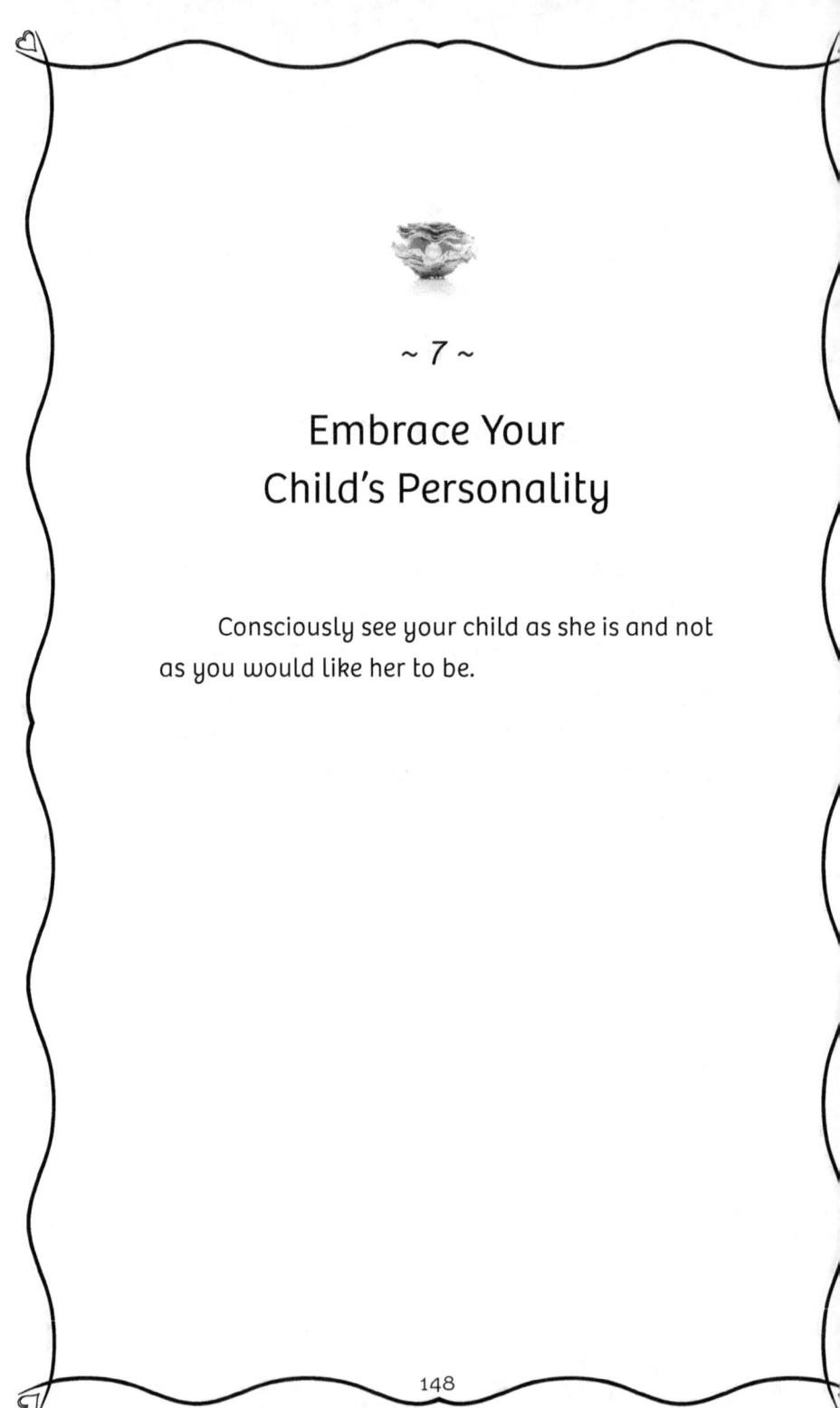

~ 7 ~

Embrace Your Child's Personality

Consciously see your child as she is and not as you would like her to be.

~ 8 ~

Treat Playtime as Precious Time

Play with your child every day. Time goes fast and soon your child will be a grown-up.

~ 9 ~

Encourage Your Child

Children have their own gifts. Encourage positive self-competition, by asking these important questions:

"Did you do your best?" "Are you happy with it?" "If not, what will you do differently next time?"

Avoid comparing your child to anyone—it's hurtful and accomplishes nothing.

~ 10 ~

Savor Each Moment like a Special Treat

Savor fully the moments you connect with your child. Look at her and engrave this picture in your mind to re-live and re-enjoy later in life.

Never take family for granted. Anything can change in a moment.

~ 11 ~

Be Open to Your Child Remembering a Past Life

If your child talks about other parents he had or a sister who died, all of which you know nothing of, don't dismiss him so quickly. For more than forty years, Dr. Ian Stevenson and Dr. Jim B. Tucker at the University of Virginia School of Medicine, Division of Perceptual Studies, have conducted research into young children's reports of a prior life.

During their field work, they interviewed over 3,000 children who claimed to have past-life memories and produced over 300 papers and fourteen books on reincarnation. Start by reading Jim Tucker's book *Life Before Life*.

~ 12 ~

Encourage Discovery Through Reading

Read aloud children's books you love. Make it fun, interesting, and playful.

Consider teaching your child about the energy of words through *The Hidden Messages in Water* or *The Secret of Water* by Masuru Emoto—you and your child will be amazed.

~ 13 ~

Promote Learning as a Fun Activity

Emphasize the learning experience and promote eagerness to learn new things every day. After school, ask your child about her friends, her teachers, her favorite activity of the day, and what she learned today.

Make learning fun.

Promote your child's natural talents and abilities. For example: "You have such a great imagination!"

"Imagination is more important than knowledge," said Albert Einstein.

~ 14 ~

Reach Out for Help

Ask for professional help when you have a problem with your child. Seek out the director of the school first because they have access to a lot of resources, as well as knowledge and experience. You can also ask a teacher, child psychologist, or speech or occupational therapist. Caregivers often love to help you without casting judgment.

~ 15 ~

During an Emotional Roller Coaster Ride, Hold on Tight

Children can go from super-happy to dramatically crying as if the world just ended to joyous again in under ten seconds. Knowing with certainty that this, too, shall pass makes handling the ups and downs easier.

Starting preschool, for example, can be challenging for both you and your child. The separation he will experience may be a bit sad and difficult at the beginning.

Another emotional time for you may be when, after a few days or weeks, your child barely says goodbye to you and runs to the playground without looking back.

Being prepared and foreseeing a future when your child feels independent, self-assured, and happy to have new friends may help you when your child is clinging onto you on his first day at school.

~ 16 ~

Seek Out Resources

Read or listen to parenting books and other materials designed to help you. *You Raising Your Child* by Dr. Michael Roizen and Dr. Mehmet Oz will make your life a lot easier.

~ 17 ~

Be Sensitive to Your Child's Fears

It's important to not play the Fear Card with our children as a disciplinary tactic, for example: "You don't want to come? I'm leaving, bye!"

You may want to say instead: "Since I have been waiting for fifteen minutes now, I am going to go, and I will come back in a little while." Then start walking like you mean it, and you will see your child following you.

This happens especially often in preschool.

~ 18 ~
Communicate with Your Preschool

Make sure you inform the appropriate party when something happens in your child's life that's unusual, or even slightly outside the normal routine: Mom is traveling, Grandma passed away, Uncle Troy is here on an extended visit, or your child went to the doctor for a checkup. This will help your child's caregivers better understand what your child may be going through.

~ 19 ~

Handle Disagreements Respectfully

If you have an issue with a teacher, a parent, a child, or anyone else at a school, contact the director and handle it without your child present. Go in with the intention of finding a solution to the problem, keeping in mind this is your child's sacred space.

~ 20 ~

Get the School's Perspective

If your child tells you about an event or activity that seems unusual or even worrisome, such as eating pizza every day for lunch or not having any friends, always double-check with the director to get an adult perspective.

~ 21 ~

Pick Proudly Your Preschool Partner

Choose a preschool close to home or work to ease your life unless you don't mind driving.

Most importantly, choose a preschool where you absolutely love the founder, the director, teachers, and the energy overall. It's all about the people. The staff will be your partners in education, you will see them every day for several years.

Pay attention to how you feel while entering and taking a tour. The vibe and the energy should be happy, exciting, and peaceful.

~ 22 ~

Prepare for Preschool like a Pro

1. Show your child her new school several days before she starts and talk to her with excitement about all the fun stuff she will do.

2. Take the time to have a good first day by sharing breakfast in a relaxed atmosphere.

3. When it's time to say goodbye on the first day, make it sweet and short without lingering and awaiting a difficult reaction.

4. Reassure your child every day as you drop her off that it will be for several hours only and that Mommy or Daddy will always come back to pick her up.

5. Take a school schedule home and talk to your child about it so she knows what to expect.

6. Reassure your child that she will have a great time playing with her friends, painting, dancing, and learning while you are at work.

7. Before school starts, meet your child's teacher and introduce your child personally.

8. Pick out the clothes to wear to school the night before, giving your child the choice.

~ 23 ~
Choose a School or Preschool that Matches Your Value System

It's important for a child to receive the same messages at home and at school.

Therefore, if you are not religious, it's not a good idea to place your child in a religious school. If you are bilingual, on the other hand, it makes sense to place your child in a bilingual school.

If you believe it's important for children to play, then choose a play-based preschool. NOTE: Knowing now the educational value of play for young children, experts recommend your child be in a play-based preschool from ages two to five. After preschool, your child will follow academic studies for the rest of his school years.

~ 24 ~

Be Part of a Village

A school should be a village to raise your child in with nurturing and clear intentions. Be active in the village and contribute to an atmosphere of love, peace, and generosity.

~ 25 ~

Be Diligent about Hand-Washing

Washing hands often with soap and water is the best way to prevent disease. It is an essential habit to instill from the moment your child starts walking and especially potty training.

Make sure you and your child always wash your hands when entering your home and always after using the bathroom.

Washing hands is not playing with water—but you can make the task fun by singing songs you invent or find online, or by using foamy soaps with interesting scents.

~ 26 ~

Talk about Body, Privacy, and Sex

Talk to your child about the privacy of her body and her friends' as well.

Explain to your child where we really come from and how she was conceived.

If your child explores the private parts of another child at school or even her own in public, explain to her: "The reason we call our private parts 'private' is to keep them to ourselves—we don't show them in public nor to our friends."

~ 27 ~

Prepare Properly for Potty-Pooping

Think of potty "training" as "potty readiness." This is a complex physiological and emotional process for children two to three years old.

You can suggest using the potty and read books about it, but let your child lead you and show you his interest so it doesn't become a power struggle. Treat it as walking—meaning a natural process that will unfold gradually at your child's own pace.

You can ask your child if she wants to wear underwear or diapers, and depending on her answer go shopping together for fun underpants. If she is potty-ready and doesn't want either, so be it. Just be sure she is wearing pants.

~ 28 ~

Encourage Friendships of Substance

Talk to you child about choosing her friends carefully based on authenticity and character traits, not hipness or coolness!

Teach her how to watch for signs of a great— and not-so-great—friendship. Positive signs include displays of love and kindness. Negative signs are competitiveness and use of humor that diminishes the other person.

About the Author

Brigitte Benchimol is an early childhood education expert, a preschool director and founder, consultant, and an author. She is a progressive thought leader and a public speaker.

For the past twenty years, she has operated three preschools in Los Angeles, California, which continue to successfully serve parents and their children. She is also a consultant to preschool owners and directors. Brigitte has written three children's books: *Discovering India, I Met Ghandi,* and *Kenya! Kenya!,* which are all part of the award-winning series *Jadyn and the Magic Bubble*. The series covers the crucial topics of multiculturalism, diversity, peace and wildlife conservation.

Pearls for Parents' Happiness

Character education and choosing happiness are the pillars of her philosophy at Creative Mind Preschool, which she founded in Hollywood, California, in 2015.

For the past ten years Brigitte has worked diligently to develop the right tools to help parents raise their children.

This latest project, *Pearls for Parents' Happiness,* offers easy-to-adopt pearls of wisdom that you can put into practice as you develop your parenting skills.

Happy Parenting!

www.ingramcontent.com/pod-product-compliance
Lightning Source LLC
Chambersburg PA
CBHW050636300426
44112CB00012B/1827